KATE BUSH

All The Top 40 Hits

Craig Halstead

Second Edition

for Aaron

BY THE SAME AUTHOR ...

Christmas Number Ones

This book details the Christmas No.1 singles in the UK from 1940 to date, and also reveals the Christmas No.2 single and Christmas No.1 album. The book also features the Christmas No.1s in five other countries, namely Australia, Germany, Ireland, the Netherlands and the United States, and is up-dated annually in January.

The 'All The Top 40 Hits' Series

This series documents, in chronological order, all the Top 40 Hit Singles and Albums by the featured artist:

ABBA
Annie Lennox (incl. Eurythmics)
Bee Gees
Blondie
Boney M.
Boy George & Culture Club
Carpenters
Chi-Lites & Stylistics
Donna Summer
Duran Duran
George Michael (incl. Wham!)
Janet Jackson
Kate Bush
Kim Wilde
Lionel Richie (incl. Commodores)
Marvin Gaye
Michael Jackson
The Jacksons (Jackson 5/Jacksons/Jermaine/La Toya/Rebbie/3T)
Olivia Newton-John
Sam Cooke & Otis Redding
Dame Shirley Bassey
Slade
Spice Girls
Tina Turner
Whitney Houston

The 'For The Record' Series

The books in this series are more comprehensive than the 'All The Top 40 Hits' volumes, and typically include: The Songs (released & unreleased), The Albums, The Home Videos, The TV Shows/Films, The Concerts, Chartography & USA/UK Chart Runs, USA Discography & UK Discography.

Donna Summer
Janet Jackson
Michael Jackson
Whitney Houston

Fiction

The James Harris Trilogy

The Secret Library
Shadow Of Death
Twist Of Fate

Cataclysm

Book 1: The First 73 Days
Book 2: A New Year

Stand Alone Novel

Tyranny

Novellas

Alone
Passion
Taboo

ACKNOWLEDGEMENTS

I would like to thank Chris Cadman, my former writing partner, for helping to make my writing dreams come true. It's incredible to think how far we have come, since we got together to compile 'The Complete Michael Jackson Discography 1972-1990', for Adrian Grant's *Off the Wall* fan magazine in 1990. Good luck with your future projects, Chris ~ I will look forward to reading them!

Chris Kimberley, it's hard to believe we have been corresponding and exchanging chart action for 30+ years! A big thank you, I will always value your friendship.

I would like to thank the online music community, who so readily share and exchange information at: Chartbusters (chartbusters.forumfree.it), ukmix (ukmix.org/forums), Haven (fatherandy2.proboards.com) & Buzzjack (buzzjack.com/forums). In particular, I would like to thank:

- 'BrainDamagell' & 'Wayne' for posting current Canadian charts on ukmix;
- 'flatdeejay' & 'ChartFreaky' for posting German chart action, and 'Indi' for answering my queries regarding Germany, on ukmix;
- 'mario' for posting Japanese chart action, and 'danavon' for answering my queries regarding Japan, on ukmix;
- 'Davidalic' for posting Spanish chart action on ukmix;
- 'Shakyfan', 'CZB', 'beatlened' & 'trebor' for posting Irish charts on ukmix;
- 'CZB' and 'janjensen' for posting Danish charts on ukmix;
- 'Hanboo' for posting and up-dating on request full UK & USA chart runs on ukmix. R.I.P., Hanboo, your posts on ukmix are sadly missed;

If you can fill any of the gaps in the chart information in this book, or have chart runs from a country not already featured in the book, I would love to hear from you. You can contact me via email at: **craig.halstead2@ntlworld.com** ~ thank you!

CONTENTS

INTRODUCTION   9

ALL THE TOP 40 SINGLES   17

THE ALMOST TOP 40 SINGLES   95

KATE'S TOP 20 SINGLES   97

SINGLES TRIVIA   101

ALL THE TOP 40 ALBUMS   111

KATE'S TOP 10 ALBUMS   173

ALBUMS TRIVIA   175

FREE CD!

PISTOLS STEVE JONES SPEAKS!

THE BAND THE TRUTH! BY ROBBIE

MOJO *The Music Magazine*

THE **ONLY** INTERVIEW!

KATE BUSH

HER GREATEST TRIUMPH
THE FULL STORY

2016
THE 50 ALBUMS YOU MUST OWN!
BOWIE, BRUCE, FRANK OCEAN AND MORE!

R.E.M., PIXIES, BLONDIE IN THE BEST THING I'VE HEARD ALL YEAR!

ALSO!
BILLY BRAGG & JOE HENRY
CHRISTINE AND THE QUEENS
ARTHUR RUSSELL
FAITH NO MORE
JAMES BOOKER
JOHNNY MARR

PLUS!
OASIS BE HERE NOW
THE MADNESS... BY NOEL GALLAGHER

THE LAST DAYS OF **PETE BURNS**

PAUL WELLER WAVES THE RED FLAG

If your CD is missing please
obtain your newsagent...
for copyright reasons the
CD is not available in some
overseas territories.

JANUARY 2017

INTRODUCTION

Catherine Bush was born in Bexleyheath in Kent, England, on 30th July 1958. Her father Robert Bush was a doctor, and her mother Hannah Bush (née Daly) was an Irish staff nurse.

As a young child, Catherine was generally known as Cathy, only becoming Kate as she grew older. Kate taught herself to play the piano, and she started to compose her own songs at the tender age of 11 years.

'The original idea,' she said, 'was to see if we (her family) could sell my songs to a publisher, not that I should be a singer or a performer or anything. We had quite modest, curious aims, so it was gradual and they were always supportive.'

Before she turned 15, Kate had written more than 50 songs and, with the help and support of her family, she recorded a vocal/piano demo tape but record companies they sent it to weren't interested.

Kate's brother John, from his time at Cambridge University, knew Ricky Hopper, who had a few contacts within the music industry. They asked him for his help, to try to place Kate's demos. One of those contacts happened to be Pink Floyd's David Gilmour who, after listening to Kate's tape, said he would like to meet her and hear her play live. Made aware how nervous Kate got, when anyone was listening to her play and sing, Gilmour initially listened secretly from an adjoining room, before making his presence known, and asking Kate to play and sing some more.

'I was absolutely terrified and trembling like a leaf,' she admitted. 'He came along to see me and he was great, such a human, kind person, and genuine.'

A month or so later, Gilmour invited Kate to his home studio, to record a few of her songs with a backing band ~ songs that included *The Man With The Child In His Eyes*. However, the resultant tape produced no immediate interest.

Kate passed ten O levels, and was revising for her mock A levels, when Gilmour booked and paid for a session for her, at George Martin's AIR studio in London's West End. She recorded three songs, *The Man With The Child In His Eyes*, *Saxophone Song* and *Davy* (the first two of which later appeared on her debut album).

'He put up the money for me to do that,' said Kate, 'which is amazing. No way could I have afforded to do something like that.'

Gilmour went further, and put together a makeshift band, to add 'oomph' to *The Man With The Child In His Eyes* and *Saxophone Song*.

Pink Floyd, who were on the EMI record label, were working on their *WISH YOU WERE HERE* album, when Gilmour took the opportunity to pass Kate's tape to Bob Mercer, who was the general manager of EMI's pop division.

Mercer was intrigued by what he heard, but it was a while before a record deal was finally agreed: Kate received an advance of £3,000 for a four year contract. However, demonstrating the label wasn't entirely convinced things would work out, EMI had the option to terminate Kate's contract at the end of the second or the third year, if they were unhappy for any reason.

Kate Bush

How To Be Invisible

ff

Kate left school after sitting her mock A levels, and *The Man With The Child In His Eyes* and *Saxophone Song* apart, which she completed in June 1975, she recorded her debut album *THE KICK INSIDE* in July and August 1977. EMI wanted to release *James And The Cold Gun* as Kate's debut single; Kate wanted to go with *Wuthering Heights*.

'It had to be the single,' she stated. 'To me it was the only one. I had to fight off a few other people's opinions but in the end they agreed with me.'

Kate attended a meeting with EMI executives, to try to put her point of view across ~ only to be told she didn't understand the market.

Upset, Kate sought a meeting with Bob Mercer, who told her he didn't come down to the studio to tell her how to do her job, so she shouldn't be trying to tell him how to do his. At that, Kate burst into tears ~ not a reaction Mercer anticipated or knew how to deal with. But, as it happened, it worked in Kate's favour.

'Frankly, I don't think there are any hits on the album,' Mercer told her, 'so we'll put *Wuthering Heights* out. It will hit a wall and then you'll understand what I'm talking about.'

Of course, *Wuthering Heights* didn't hit a wall ~ it went to no.1 in the UK, and stayed there for four weeks. Not only that, it broke Kate internationally as well, topping the charts in several countries around the world. The follow-up, *The Man With The Child In His Eyes*, was a hit as well, and Kate's debut album *THE KICK INSIDE* went on to sell over a million copies in the UK alone ~ unheard of, for a female artist who had composed every single song on her album, as Kate had.

Over the years, Kate has been nominated for 13 Brit awards, including eight for Best British Female, and three Grammy Awards. Her unique and experimental musical style was recognised in 2002, when she was awarded an Ivor Novello Award for her Outstanding Contribution to British Music, and in the 2013 New Years Honours she was appointed a CBE, for her services to music.

In December 2018, Kate published her first book, *How To Be Invisible*, an illustrated collection of her lyrics.

All The Top 40 Hits

For the purposes of this book, to qualify as a Top 40 hit, a single or album must have entered the Top 40 singles/albums chart in at least one of the following countries: Australia, Austria, Belgium, Canada, Finland, France, Germany, Ireland, Italy, Japan, the Netherlands, New Zealand, Norway, South Africa, Spain, Sweden, Switzerland, the United Kingdom and the United States of America.

The Top 40 singles and albums are detailed chronologically, according to the date they first entered the chart in one or more of the featured countries. Each Top 40 single and album is illustrated and the catalogue numbers and release dates are detailed, for the UK, followed by the chart action in each featured country, including any chart re-entries. Where full chart runs are unavailable, peak position and weeks on the chart are given.

For both singles and albums, the main listing is followed by 'The Almost Top 40 Singles/Albums', which gives an honorable mention to Kate's singles/albums that peaked between no.41 and no.50 in one or more countries. There is also a points-based list of Kate's Top 20 Singles and Top 10 Albums, plus a fascinating 'Trivia' section at the end of each section which looks at the most successful singles and albums in each of the featured countries.

The Charts

The charts from an increasing number of countries are now freely available online, and for many countries it is possible to research weekly chart runs. Although this book focuses on Top 50 hits, longer charts runs are included where available, up to the Top 100 for countries where a Top 100 or longer is published.

Nowadays, charts are compiled and published on a weekly basis – in the past, however, some countries published charts on a bi-weekly or monthly basis, and most charts listed far fewer titles than they do today. There follows a summary of the current charts from each country featured in this book, together with relevant online resources and chart books.

Australia
Current charts: Top 100 Singles & Top 100 Albums.
Online resources: current weekly Top 50 Singles & Albums, but no archive, at **ariacharts.com.au**; archive of complete weekly charts dating back to 2001 at **pandora.nla.gov.au/tep/23790**; searchable archive of Top 50 Singles & Albums dating back to 1988 at **australian-charts.com**.
Books: 'Australian Chart Book 1970-1992' & 'Australian Chart Book 1993-2009' by David Kent.

Austria
Current charts: Top 75 Singles & Top 75 Albums.
Online resources: current weekly charts and a searchable archive dating back to 1965 for singles and 1973 for albums at **austriancharts.at**.

Belgium
Current charts: Top 50 Singles & Top 200 Albums for two different regions, Flanders (the Dutch speaking north of the country) and Wallonia (the French speaking south).
Online resources: current weekly charts and a searchable archive dating back to 1956 for singles and 1995 for albums at **ultratop.be**.
Book: '*Het Belgisch Hitboek – 40 Jaar Hits In Vlaanderen*' by Robert Collin.
Note: the information in this book for Belgium relates to the Flanders region.

Canada
Current charts: Hot 100 Singles & Top 100 Albums.
Online resources: weekly charts and a searchable archive of weekly charts from the Nielsen SoundScan era at **billboard.com/biz** (subscription only); incomplete archive of weekly RPM charts dating back to 1964 for singles and 1967 for albums at **https://www.bac-lac.gc.ca/eng/Pages/home.aspx** (search 'RPM charts'). Scans of RPM Weekly magazine can be viewed at **https://3345.ca/rpm-magazine/** and **https://worldradiohistory.com/RPM.htm** (RPM folded in 2000).
Book: 'The Canadian Singles Chart Book 1975-1996' by Nanda Lwin.

Denmark
Current Charts: Top 40 Singles & Albums.
Online resources: weekly charts at **hitlisten.nu**, and formally an archive dating back to 2001 at **danishcharts.com**. No archive currently exists for charts before 2001. 'CZB' has posted weekly Top 20s from September 1994 to December 1999 on **ukmix.org**, and 'janjensen' has posted singles charts from January 1977 onwards on the same forum.

Finland
Current charts: Top 20 Singles & Top 50 Albums.
Online resources: current weekly charts and a searchable archive dating back to 1995 at **finnishcharts.com**.
Book: '*Sisältää Hitin*' by Timo Pennanen.

France
Current charts: Top 200 Singles & Top 200 Albums.
Online resources: current weekly and archive charts dating back to 2001 can be found at **snepmusique.com**; a searchable archive dating back to 1984 for singles and 1997 for albums is at **lescharts.com**; searchable archive for earlier/other charts at **infodisc.fr**.
Book: '*Hit Parades 1950-1998*' by Daniel Lesueur.
Note: Compilation albums were excluded from the main chart until 2008, when a Top 200 Comprehensive chart was launched.

Germany
Current charts: Top 100 Singles & Top 100 Albums.
Online resources: current weekly and archive charts dating back to 1977 can be found at **offiziellecharts.de/charts**.
Books: '*Deutsche Chart Singles 1956-1980*', '*Deutsche Chart Singles 1981-90*' & '*Deutsche Chart Singles 1991-1995*' published by Taurus Press.

Ireland
Current charts: Top 100 Singles & Top 100 Albums.

Online resources: current weekly charts are published at IRMA (**irma.ie**); there is a searchable archive for Top 30 singles (entry date, peak position and week on chart only) at **irishcharts.ie**; an annual Irish Chart Thread has been published annually from 2007 to date, plus singles charts from 1967 to 1999 and album charts for 1993, 1995-6 and 1999, have been published at ukmix (**ukmix.org**); weekly album charts from March 2003 to date can be found at **acharts.us/ireland_albums_top_75**.
Note: the information presented in this book is for singles only.

Italy
Current charts: Top 100 Singles & Top 100 Albums.
Online resources: weekly charts and a weekly chart archive dating back to 2005 at **fimi.it**; a searchable archive of Top 20 charts dating back to 2000 at **italiancharts.com**; pre-2000 information has been posted at ukmix (**ukmix.org**).
Books: *Musica e Dischi Borsa Singoli 1960-2019* & *Musica e Dischi Borsa Album 1964-2019* by Guido Racca.
Note: as the FIMI-Neilsen charts didn't start until 1995, the information detailed in this book is from the Musica & Dischi chart.

Japan
Current charts: Top 200 Singles & Top 300 Albums.
Online resources: current weekly charts (in Japanese) at **oricon.co.jp/rank**; selected information is available on the Japanese Chart/The Newest Charts and Japanese Chart/The Archives threads at **ukmix.org**.

Netherlands
Current charts: Top 100 Singles & Top 100 Albums.
Online resources: current weekly charts and a searchable archive dating back to 1956 for singles and 1969 for albums at **dutchcharts.nl**.

New Zealand
Current charts: Top 40 Singles & Top 40 Albums.
Online resources: current weekly charts and a searchable archive dating back to 1975 at **nztop40.co.nz**.
Book: 'The Complete New Zealand Music Charts 1966-2006' by Dean Scapolo.

Norway
Current charts: Top 20 Singles & Top 40 Albums.
Online resources: current weekly charts and a searchable archive dating back to 1958 for singles and 1967 for albums at **norwegiancharts.com**.

South Africa
Current charts: no official charts.
Online resources: none known.
Book: 'South Africa Chart Book' by Christopher Kimberley.

Notes: the singles chart was discontinued in early 1989, as singles were no longer being manufactured in significant numbers. The albums chart only commenced in December 1981, and was discontinued in 1995, following re-structuring of the South African Broadcasting Corporation.

Spain
Current charts: Top 50 Singles & Top 100 Albums.
Online resources: current weekly charts and a searchable archive dating back to 2005 at **spanishcharts.com**.
Book: *'Sólo éxitos 1959-2002 Año a Año'* by Fernando Salaverri.

Sweden
Current charts: Top 60 Singles & Top 100 Albums.
Online resources: current weekly charts and a searchable archive dating back to 1975 at **swedishcharts.com**.
Note: before 1975, a weekly Top 20 *Kvällstoppen* charts was published, which was a sales-based, mixed singles/albums chart.

Switzerland
Current charts: Top 75 Singles & Top 100 Albums.
Online resources: current weekly charts and a searchable archive dating back to 1968 for singles and 1983 for albums at **hitparade.ch**.

UK
Current Charts: Top 100 Singles & Top 200 Albums.
Online resources: current weekly and archive charts dating back to 1960 at **officialcharts.com**; weekly charts are posted on a number of music forums, including ukmix (**ukmix.org**), Haven (**fatherandy2.proboards.com**) and Buzzjack (**buzzjack.com**).
Note: weekly Top 200 album charts are only available via subscription from UK ChartsPlus (**ukchartsplus.co.uk**).

USA
Current charts: Hot 100 Singles & Billboard 200 Albums.
Online resources: current and archive weekly charts are available at **billboard.com** (archive charts via subscription only); weekly charts are also posted on a number of music forums, including ukmix (**ukmix.org**), Haven (**fatherandy2.proboards.com**) and Buzzjack (**buzzjack.com**).
Note: the Hot 100 singles chart wasn't launched until August 1958; before this date, the most popular chart was Billboard's Best Seller in Stores, which has been used for the pre-Hot 100 era.

RECORD COLLECTOR PRESENTS
KATE BUSH

DEEPER UNDERSTANDING

ALL THE LOVE
FANS ON WHAT
KATE MEANS
TO THEM

**ALL WE EVER
LOOK FOR**
HER 40 MOST
COLLECTABLE
RELEASES

£8.49

COLLECTING KATE
COMPREHENSIVE
UK DISCOGRAPHY,
MEMORABILIA, UK
AND WORLDWIDE
RARITIES & MORE

FROM THE
ARCHIVES OF
**RECORD
COLLECTOR**

PLUS: CLASSIC FEATURES EVERY ALBUM REVISITED
HER GLORIOUS LIVE COMEBACK **UNPUBLISHED PHOTOS**

All The Top 40 Singles

1 ~ Wuthering Heights

UK: EMI 2719 (1978).
  B-side: *Kite*.

11.02.78: 42-27-13-5-**1-1-1-1**-3-8-15-28-x-75

Pos	LW	Title, Artist		Peak Pos	WoC
1	5 ↑	**WUTHERING HEIGHTS** KATE BUSH	EMI	1	5
2	1 ↓	**TAKE A CHANCE ON ME** ABBA	EPIC	1	6
3	2 ↓	**COME BACK MY LOVE** DARTS	MAGNET	2	7

6.09.14: 57

Australia
17.04.78: peaked at no.**1** (3), charted for 20 weeks
29.04.12: 39

Austria
15.10.78: **17** (monthly)

Belgium
18.03.78: 27-18-18-9-**6**-7-7-8-12-16-20

Denmark
12.01.79: **5-5-5**-6-8-10

Finland
04.78: peaked at no.**2**, charted for 4 months

France
21.04.78: peaked at no.**14**, charted for 24 weeks
28.04.12: 75-91

Germany
10.04.78: 19-20-13-12-**11-11**-12-16-13-13-17-21-17-21-29-29-43-44-42-50-49

Ireland
23.03.78: **1-1-1**-2-2-8-19

Italy
3.06.78: peaked at no.**1** (1), charted for 26 weeks

Netherlands
25.03.78: 6-5-**3**-6-8-8-19-26

New Zealand
9.04.78: 35-7-2-2-**1-1-1-1-1**-2-2-6-7-9-13-16-21-25-31-36

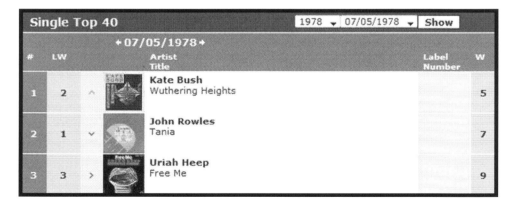

Norway
15.04.78: 9-8-**7**-9-9-9-9-8-8-**7**

South Africa
15.07.78: peaked at no.**3**, charted for 11 weeks

Spain
25.09.78: peaked at no.**10**, charted for 9 weeks

Sweden
21.04.78: 12-16-14-13-15-19-7-**6**-7-10-19-16

Switzerland
1.07.78: 14-12-9-9-**8-8**-10-10-10-**8**-11-14-14

Wuthering Heights was, of course, inspired by Emily Brontë's 1847 novel with the same title. However, when she wrote the song, Kate had only read a small part of the book and was more familiar with the 1970 film adaptation of *Wuthering Heights*, which starred Timothy Dalton as Heathcliff and Anna Calder-Marshall as Cathy.

'It's about the end of the film where Cathy has actually died and she's coming back as a spirit across the moors to come and get Heathcliff again,' said Kate. 'And it just struck me very strongly because it shows a lot about human beings and how if they can't get what they want, they will go to such extremes in order to do it. This is exactly what she did. She wouldn't even be alone when she was dead. She had to come back and get him. I just found it really amazing.'

Coincidentally, Kate and Emily Brontë shared the same birthday ~ 30th July ~ and Kate was known as Cathy when she was younger.

'I loved writing it,' said Kate. 'It was a real challenge to précis the whole mood of a book into such a short piece of prose. Also, when I was a child I was always called Cathy not Kate, and I just found myself able to relate to her as a character. It's so important to put yourself in the role of the person in a song. There's no half measures. When I sing that song I am Cathy.'

Kate recorded 13 songs for her debut album, but she always knew she wanted to release *Wuthering Heights* as the first single ~ however, she had to fight her corner, before her record company EMI gave in, and agreed to go with *Wuthering Heights* instead of their choice, *James And The Cold Gun*. Even so, Kate wasn't expecting her debut single to be as well received and successful as it was.

'I was amazed at the response though,' she later admitted, 'truly overwhelmed!'

Wuthering Heights was released in the UK on 4th November 1977 and, initially, it did nothing. It wasn't until 11th February 1978, when the single finally crept into the chart at a lowly no.42.

Four weeks later, *Wuthering Heights* hit no.1, deposing ABBA's *Take A Chance On Me*. The single topped the chart for four weeks, and was the first chart topping single by a British female singer-songwriter with one of her own songs. *Wuthering Heights* was the no.10 best-selling single of 1978 in the UK.

Kate filmed two music videos to promote *Wuthering Heights*, both of which she choreographed herself.

In the first, Kate is seen wearing a white dress, and performing the song in a dark room with swirling white mist around her feet. This version was aimed at the UK and continental Europe, while the second promo was aimed at the North American market. In this music video, Kate is wearing a red dress, and is seen dancing in a grassy area with Scots pine trees in the background.

Outside the UK, *Wuthering Heights* hit no.1 in Australia, Ireland, Italy and New Zealand, and achieved no.2 in Finland, no.3 in the Netherlands and South Africa, no.5 in Denmark, no.6 in Belgium and Sweden, no.7 in Norway, no.8 in Switzerland, no.10 in Spain, no.11 in Germany, no.14 in France and no.17 in Austria.

In Brazil, *Wuthering Heights* was the lead song on a 4-track EP titled *4 Sucessos*, which also featured *The Man With The Child In His Eyes*, *Moving* and *Oh To Be In Love*.

Kate re-recorded *Wuthering Heights* for her 1986 compilation album, *THE WHOLE STORY* ~ this version was also issued as the B-side of her single, *Experiment IV*.

2 ~ The Man With The Child In His Eyes

UK: EMI 2806 (1978).
 B-side: *Moving*.

10.06.78: 60-30-17-7-**6**-9-9-15-24-35-70

Australia
17.07.78: peaked at no.**22**, charted for 19 weeks

Ireland
30.06.78: 12-**3**-7-14-11-24

Netherlands
24.06.78: 38-38-49-35-25-**23**-27-28-43-44
26.11.11: 99

New Zealand
23.07.78: 40-**36**

USA
17.02.79: 88-86-**85**-96

Kate wrote *The Man With The Child In His Eyes* three years before her debut album, *THE KICK INSIDE* was released.
 'I wrote that when I was sixteen,' she said. 'The inspiration for *The Man With The Child In His Eyes* was really just a particular thing that happened when I went to the

piano. The piano just started speaking to me. It was a theory that I had had for a while that I just observed in most of the men that I know: the fact that they just are little boys inside and how wonderful it is that they manage to retain this magic.'

The Man With The Child In His Eyes was one of the songs Kate recorded with Pink Floyd's David Gilmour, before she signed with EMI. Kate confirmed the photograph of her younger self, as featured on the single's sleeve, was taken by her brother, John.

After *Wuthering Heights*, many observers dismissed Kate as a novelty act, and predicted she would be a one-hit wonder. So, following the wholly unique sounding *Wuthering Heights*, *The Man With The Child In His Eyes* was an astute choice as Kate's second single, as arguably it was the least 'weird' sounding song on her debut album, being a gentle, tender ballad.

Kate added a 'He's here …' introduction to the single version of *The Man With The Child In His Eyes*, which was absent from the album version. She promoted the release with a simple, yet effective, music video.

'The song dictated it,' said Kate. 'It was a very intimate song about a young girl almost voicing her inner thoughts, not really to anyone, but rather to herself. And it just started off where I sat down on the floor, cross-legged, and getting ready to work out some ideas to the routine with the music on. And my brother Jay (John) came in and saw me sitting there and said, "Why don't you just keep it like that?".'

The Man With The Child In His Eyes couldn't match the success of *Wuthering Heights*, but it did give Kate her second Top 10 success in the UK, where it peaked at no.6. The single charted three places higher in Ireland, and achieved no.22 in Australia, no.23 in the Netherlands and no.36 in New Zealand.

Although it peaked at a lowly no.85 during a brief, four week chart run, *The Man With The Child In His Eyes* gave Kate her first Hot 100 hit in the United States, thus outperforming *Wuthering Heights*, which had failed to chart.

3 ~ Hammer Horror

UK: EMI 2887 (1978).
  B-side: *Coffee Homeground.*

11.11.78: 73-49-**44**-54-61-65

Australia
20.11.78: peaked at no.**17**, charted for 14 weeks

Ireland
24.11.78: 14-**10**-14

Netherlands
2.12.78: 31-**25**-36-32-27

New Zealand
3.12.78: **21-21-21-21-21-21-21**-29-35

Contrary to the song's title, Kate wasn't inspired to write *Hammer Horror* by the old horror movies made the Hammer Films.
  'The song was inspired by seeing James Cagney playing the part of Lon Chaney playing the hunchback,' said Kate. 'He was an actor in an actor in an actor, rather like Chinese boxes, and that's what I was trying to create.'
  The film in question was the 1957 biographical film, *Man Of A Thousand Faces*, which is about an actor and his friend. The actor is about to realise his dream, to play the lead role in a production of *The Hunchback Of Notre Dame*, when after many rehearsals he

dies. Then, when the actor's friend takes over his role, the dead man comes back to haunt him.

Kate explained, 'And the actor is saying, "Leave me alone, because it wasn't my fault ~ I have to take this part, but I'm wondering if it's the right thing to do because the ghost is not going to leave me alone and is really freaking me out. Every time I look round a corner he's there, he never disappears.".'

Kate recorded *Hammer Horror* for her second album, *LIONHEART*, and in most countries it was released as the lead single.

'Making the video of *Hammer Horror* was the first time I had worked with a dancer,' said Kate. 'I wanted to do something different with it, using a dancer, and I was sitting in a hotel room in Australia when it suddenly came to me ~ the whole routine happened before my eyes ~ and the next morning at 9.00 a.m. the dancer turned up to start work. We'd never met before, and in ten minutes we were having to throw each other around. He was so inspiring that we did the video that same afternoon.'

Whereas Kate's first two singles went Top 10 in the UK, *Hammer Horror* failed to enter the Top 40, peaking at a disappointing no.44. The single did, however, achieve Top 40 status in several countries, peaking at no.10 in Ireland, no.17 in Australia, no.21 in New Zealand and no.25 in the Netherlands.

4 ~ Wow

UK: EMI 2911 (1979).
  B-side: *Fullhouse*.

17.03.79: 61-35-23-27-**14-14-14**-17-45-69

Ireland
30.03.79: 27-**17**-24-x-25-23-29

Kate wrote and recorded *Wow* for her second album, *LIONHEART*.

'*Wow* is a song about the music business,' said Kate, 'not just rock music but show business in general, including acting and theatre. People say that the music business is about rip-offs, the rat race, competition, strain, people trying to cut you down, and so on, and though that's all there, there's also the magic. It was sparked off when I sat down to try and write a Pink Floyd song, something spacey, though I'm not surprised no-one has picked that up. It's not really recognisable as that, in the same way as people haven't noticed that *Kite* is a Bob Marley song, and *Don't Push Your Foot On The Heartbrake* is a Patti Smith song.'

Kate's music video for *Wow* was censored by the BBC, as the promo was considered too risqué ~ in it, Kate patted her own buttocks while singing 'He's too busy hitting the vaseline'.

In the UK, *Wow* charted thirty places higher than *Hammer Horror* had managed, peaking at no.14. The single was also a no.17 hit in Ireland but, surprisingly, it missed the charts in most countries where it was released.

KATE BUSH

her new single is

WOW
EMI 2911

taken from her album
LIONHEART
EMA 787

See her on Tour
APRIL

3 LIVERPOOL, EMPIRE	10 MANCHESTER, APOLLO
4 BIRMINGHAM, HIPPODROME	12 SUNDERLAND, EMPIRE
6 OXFORD, NEW THEATRE	13 EDINBURGH, USHER HALL
7 SOUTHAMPTON, GAUMONT	16 LONDON, PALLADIUM
9 BRISTOL, HIPPODROME	17 LONDON, PALLADIUM
	18 LONDON, PALLADIUM

In Canada, *Wow* was issued on translucent yellow vinyl, and came with a unique 7"
sleeve ~ however, despite this it wasn't a hit.

Kate performed *Wow*, when she appeared as a guest on the TV special, *ABBA In
Switzerland*, in April 1979.

KATE BUSH

TOUR OF LIFE

MANCHESTER 1979

MANCHESTER APOLLO, MANCHESTER, UK 10TH APRIL 1979

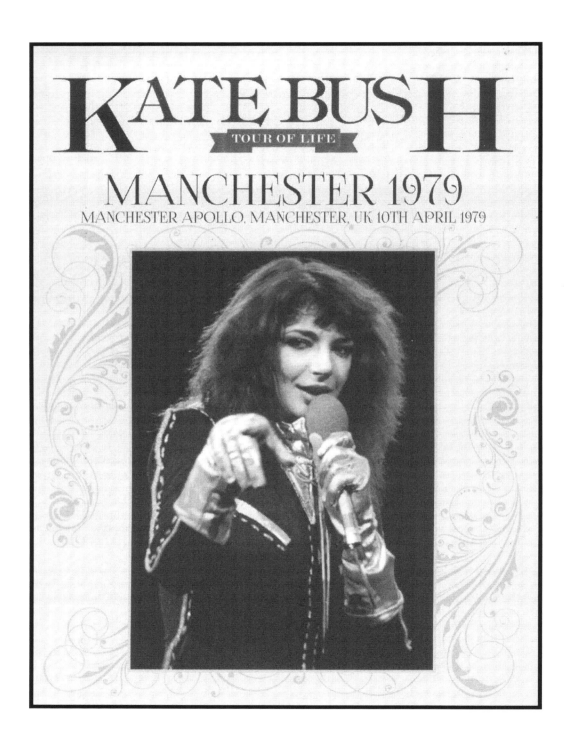

5 ~ On Stage EP

UK: EMI MIEP 2991 (1979).
    Tracks: *Them Heavy People/Don't Push Your Foot On The Heartbrake/James And The Cold Gun/L'Amour Looks Something Like You*

15.09.79: 35-27-23-11-**10**-13-25-52-73

Canada
9.04.83: 96-72-64-**57-57**-66-74-81 (Album chart)

Ireland
7.10.79: 24-18-**15**-28 (*Them Heavy People*)

Japan
5.10.79: peaked at no.**58**, charted for 4 weeks (LP chart)

Netherlands
13.10.79: 33-36-26-**17**-19-18-29-37

The four tracks on Kate's *On Stage* EP were recorded at London's Hammersmith Odeon on 13th May 1979, during her Tour Of Life concert tour.
    Kate originally recorded *Them Heavy People, James And The Cold Gun* and *L'Amour Looks Something Like You* for her *THE KICK INSIDE* album, while *Don't Push Your Foot On The Handbrake* featured on her second album, *LIONHEART*. In most countries, *Them Heavy People* was promoted as the EP's lead track.

'The idea for *Heavy People* came when I was just sitting one day in my parents' house,' said Kate. 'I heard the phrase "Rolling the ball" in my head, and I thought that it would be a good way to start a song, so I ran in to the piano and played it and got the chords down. I then worked on it from there … I always felt that *Heavy People* should be a single, but I just had a feeling that it shouldn't be a second single, although a lot of people wanted that.'

Originally, in the UK, the *On Stage* EP was issued a double, gatefold pack of two 7" singles and a 12" single ~ however, the double pack was quickly replaced with one gatefold 7" single featuring all four songs.

The *On Stage* EP achieved no.10 in the UK and no.17 in the Netherlands. In Ireland, where only *Them Heavy People* was listed, the single charted at no.15.

In Canada and Japan, the *On Stage* EP was classed as an album rather than a single, so charted on the album charts ~ it peaked at no.57 and no.58, respectively.

Games Without Frontiers

UK: Charisma CB 354 (1980).
  B-side: *The Start/I Don't Remember* (Peter Gabriel).

9.02.80: 48-38-25-17-8-**4**-6-9-22-33-53

Australia
19.05.80: peaked at no.**44**, charted for 22 weeks

Germany
12.05.80: 45-44-57-56-**36**-53-46-48-63-65-x-69

Ireland
30.03.80: 5-**3**-6-15

Sweden
18.04.80: 19-**17**

USA
16.08.80: 90-80-70-62-54-**48-48**-61-74-89-100

Games Without Frontiers was composed by Peter Gabriel, and he recorded the song ~
with Kate on backing vocals ~ for his self-titled 1980 album.

The song's title referred to the popular European TV game show, *Jeux Sans Frontières* (French for 'Games Without Borders') ~ the British version of the show was titled *It's A Knockout*.

'It seemed to have several layers to it', said Peter Gabriel. 'I just began playing in a somewhat light-hearted fashion ~ Hans and Lottie ...' ~ so it looked, on the surface, as just kids. The names themselves are meaningless, but they do have certain associations with them. So it's almost like a little kids activity room. Underneath that, you have the TV programme sort of nationalism, territorialism, competitiveness that underlies all that assembly of jolly people.'

Games Without Frontiers opens with Kates singing '*Jeux Sans Frontières*' four times, before Peter Gabriel makes an appearance, and she repeats the same phrase repeatedly throughout the song ~ she didn't, however, appear in the accompanying music video.

Games Without Frontiers was released as the lead single from *PETER GABRIEL*, and achieved no.3 in Ireland, no.4 in the UK, no.17 in Sweden, no.36 in Germany, no.44 in Australia and no.48 in the United States.

6 ~ Breathing

UK: EMI 5058 (1980).
  B-side: *The Empty Bullring*.

26.04.80: 44-29-26-19-**16**-30-37

Netherlands
24.05.80: 49-**44**-49

Kate wrote and recorded *Breathing* for her third album, *NEVER FOR EVER*, which was released in 1980.

  '*Breathing* is a warning and plea from a future spirit to try and save mankind and his planet from irretrievable destruction' said Kate. 'It's about a baby still in the mother's womb at the time of a nuclear fallout, but it's more of a spiritual being, it has all its senses: sight, smell, touch, taste and hearing, and it knows what is going on outside the mother's womb, and yet it wants desperately to carry on living, as we all do of course.'

  Breathing was released as the lead single from *NEVER FOR EVER*, and rose to no.16 in the UK. However, apart from charting at no.44 in the Netherlands, the single flopped in most countries ~ not that Kate was at all disappointed.

  'I think it did incredibly well,' she said. 'It got to number sixteen in the singles charts in this country. And it was without any promotion and everyone thought, gosh, it's far too uncommercial, but I think sixteen is pretty good. And also what is nice is that, although in a way it didn't really get that much attention at the time, it's one of those tracks that people are still talking about now, even though they may have ignored it when it first came out.'

No Self Control

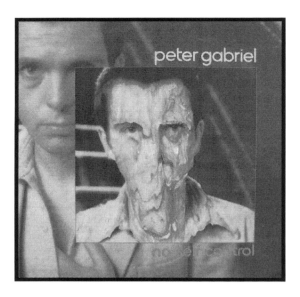

UK: Charisma CB 360 (1980).
  B-side: *Lead A Normal Life* (Peter Gabriel).

10.05.80: 58-44-42-**33**-54-56

No Self Control was written by Peter Gabriel, and he recorded the songs for his self-titled 1980 album.

   No Self Control was released as the follow-up to *Games Without Frontiers* and, as she had with *Games Without Frontiers*, Kate contributed backing vocals to *No Self Control*. However, her second collaboration with Peter Gabriel wasn't nearly as successful as the first, and *No Self Control* only managed no.33 in the UK and wasn't a hit anywhere else.

7 ~ Babooshka

UK: EMI 5085 (1980).
  B-side: *Ran Tan Waltz.*

5.07.80: 63-16-7-7-**5**-6-12-22-41-68

Australia
8.09.80: peaked at no.**2**, charted for 21 weeks

France
3.10.80: peaked at no.**4**, charted for 27 weeks

Germany
15.09.80: 59-43-27-24-26-23-34-24-18-18-20-20-**14**-24-26-29-36-31-31-33-34-41-49-58-
  64-75

Ireland
17.08.80: 7-**5**-13

Italy
27.09.80: peaked at no.**6**, charted for 20 weeks

Netherlands
9.08.80: 41-30-30-25-25-**24**-45-46

New Zealand
31.11.80: 31-15-10-**8-8-8-8**-13-16-24-22-44-38

Norway
20.09.80: 8-7-6-**4**-5-**4**-7-10

South Africa
4.10.80: peaked at no.**12**, charted for 8 weeks

Kate wrote and recorded *Babooshka* for her third album, *NEVER FOR EVER*.

Although Kate later admitted she didn't know it at the time, Babooshka (or Babushka) means Grandmother in Russian.

'It's also a headdress that people wear,' she said, 'but when I wrote the song it was just a name that literally came into my mind, I've presumed I've got it from a fairy story I'd read when I was a child, and after having written the song a series of incredible coincidences happened where I'd turned on the television and there was Donald Swan singing about Babooshka. So I thought, "well, there's got to be someone who's actually called Babooshka".'

The song tells the story of a woman who dresses as a highwayman, and entices her lover, in order to test his devotion to her. Kate, wearing a black bodysuit and veil, explored this theme further in the music video, in which she played the jealous wife.

Babooshka was issued as the second single from *NEVER FOR EVER*. After the relatively poor sales of *Breathing*, *Babooshka* was a major success in many countries. In the UK, the single added to Kate's growing tally of Top 10 hits, peaking at no.5. The single fared even better in Australia, where it rose to no.2.

Elsewhere, *Babooshka* achieved no.4 in France and Norway, no.5 in Ireland, no.6 in Italy, no.8 in New Zealand, no.12 in South Africa, no.14 in Germany and no.24 in the Netherlands.

8 ~ Army Dreamers

UK: EMI 5106 (1980).
  B-side: *Delius/Passing Through Air.*

4.10.80: 57-33-26-26-**16**-17-25-29-68

Ireland
19.10.80: 22-**14**-16-19-19-22-29

Netherlands
8.11.80: 30-**25**-35-33-38-38-35-50

Kate wrote and recorded *Army Dreamers* for her third album, *NEVER FOR EVER.*
  '*Army Dreamers* is about a grieving mother who, through the death of her soldier boy, questions her motherhood,' said Kate. 'I'm not slagging off the army, it's just so sad that there are kids who have no O levels and nothing to do but become soldiers, and it's not really what they want. That's what frightens me.'
  Army Dreamers is the first song Kate actually wrote in the studio, and she was quick to stress the song wasn't specifically about the ongoing troubles in Ireland at the time.
  'It's just putting the case of a mother in these circumstances,' she said, 'how incredibly sad it is for her ~ how she feels she should have been able to prevent it.'
  Kate dressed in dark green camouflage fatigues for the music video, which opened with a close-up of her holding a child. The child walks away and returns as a soldier, and towards the end of the promo, when Kate reaches for the soldier he disappears ~ and, finally, Kate is blown up.

'For me that's the closest that I've got to a little bit of film.' she said, 'and it was very pleasing for me to watch the ideas I'd thought of actually working beautifully. Watching it on the screen, it really was a treat, that one. I think that's the first time ever with anything I've done I can actually sit back and say, "I liked that".'

Released as the follow-up to *Babooshka* in most countries, *Army Dreamers* equalled the no.16 peak achieved by *Breathing* in the UK. The single charted two places higher in Ireland, and achieved no.25 in the Netherlands, but it failed to chart in most countries.

9 ~ December Will Be Magic Again

UK: EMI 5121 (1980).
 B-side: *Warm And Soothing*.

6.12.80: 39-**29**-30-32-32-36-74

Germany
5.01.81: 74-66-75-**55**-72

Ireland
14.12.80: 17-**15**-21-21-24

Kate originally wrote the festive-themed *December Will Be Magic Again* in 1979, and she recorded the song at London's Abbey Road Studios. She re-visited the song again in 1980, before releasing it as a non-album single.

 Unusually, Kate didn't film a music video for *December Will Be Magic Again*, and as a result it didn't attract the attention it might otherwise have done. Nevertheless, the single charted at no.15 in Ireland, no.29 in the UK and no.55 in Germany.

 Nowadays, thanks to streaming 'sales', many festive hits return to the charts year after year after year, but the lack of a music video and the fact it isn't featured on most festive streaming lists means *December Will Be Magic Again* isn't one of them, and it has largely been forgotten by most people.

ISSN 0144 5804

JULY 11, 1981. 30p

BAUHAUS • SAMSON

RECORD MIRROR

KATE BUSH exclusive interview

SQUEEZE is that American

Kid Creole/Coati Mundi
Me and Pop and I

Spring collection-fashion winners

JIM STEINMAN • ICEHOUSE • JOE JACKSON

10 ~ Sat In Your Lap

UK: EMI 5201 (1981).
  B-side: *Lord Of The Reedy River*.

11.07.81: 26-15-**11**-13-18-29-35

Australia
19.10.81: **93**

France
17.09.82: **72**

Ireland
19.07.81: 29-**18**-20-19

Italy
25.07.81: peaked at no.**25**, charted for 2 weeks

Netherlands
1.08.81: 50-47-**32**

Initially, Kate wrote and recorded *Sat In Your Lap* as a one-off single ~ it was released more than a year ahead of her fourth album, *THE DREAMING*.

  '*Sat In Your Lap* is very much a search for knowledge,' said Kate, 'and about the kind of people who really want to have knowledge but can't be bothered to do the things that they should in order to get it. So they're sitting there saying how nice it would be to have this or to do that without really desiring to do the things it takes you to get it.'

Given how far ahead of her new album it had been released, Kate didn't plan on including *Sat In Your Lap* on *THE DREAMING*.

'We weren't going to put it on initially,' she confirmed, 'because we thought it had been a single such a long time ago, but a lot of people used to ask me if we were putting *Sat In Your Lap* on the album and I'd say no, and they would say. "Oh, why not?" and they'd be quite disappointed. So, as the album's completion date got nearer and nearer, I eventually relented. I re-mixed the track and we put it on. I'm so glad I did now, because it says so much about side one, with its up-tempo beat and heavy drum rhythms ~ it's perfect for the opening track.'

Kate promoted *Sat In Your Lap* with a 'fun' music video.

'I don't think we felt it was a serious video, you know,' she said, 'it's meant to be fun. We thought the roller skates needed an airing!'

Sat In Your Lap achieved no.11 in the UK, no.18 in Ireland, no.25 in Italy and no.32 in the Netherlands, and it was a minor hit in Australia and France.

Kate recorded a cover ~ her first ~ of Donovan's *Lord Of The Reedy River* for the B-side of *Sat In Your Lap*. The song originally featured on Donovan's 1971 album, *HMS DONOVAN*.

11 ~ Suspended In Gaffa

UK: Not released.

France: EMI 2C 008-64979 (1982).
  B-side: *Dreamtime (Instrumental)*.

24.09.82: peaked at no.**33**, charted for 16 weeks

Netherlands
8.01.83: **50**

Kate wrote and recorded *Suspended In Gaffa* for her fourth album, *THE DREAMING*.

The song's lyrics revolve around seeing something you really want, God in this case, and then never being able to see it or experience it ever again.

Not counting *Sat In Your Lap*, *Suspended In Gaffa* was released as the second single from *THE DREAMING*, after the title track, in Australasia and continental Europe only. In the UK and Ireland, *There Goes A Tenner* was preferred.

Although it wasn't a major hit, *Suspended In Gaffa* did at least achieve Top 40 status in one country, which is more than *The Dreaming* or *There Goes A Tenner* managed. The single rose to no.33 in France, and spent a solitary week at no.50 in the Netherlands.

Ne T'Enfuis Pas (French for 'Don't Run Away'), the B-side of *Suspended In Gaffa* in some countries and the B-side of *There Goes A Tenner* in the UK, was released as a single in its own right in Canada and France, but it wasn't a hit.

Ne T'Enfuis Pas was remastered and reissued as a 12" single in France in 2019 but, once again, it failed to chart. In the UK, sufficient copies were sold via HMV and other record stores to send the single to no.1 on the Vinyl Singles chart (where it was misspelled *Ne T'En Fui Pas*, as it had been when it was issued as the B-side of *Suspended in Gaffa* and *There Goes A Tenner*).

Pos	LW	Title, Artist		Peak Pos	WoC
1	16 ↑	**NE T'EN FUI PAS** KATE BUSH	PARLOPHONE	1	2
2	1 ↓	**TAKE ON ME** A-HA	WEA	1	10
3	New	**OUT OF THE WOODS** SMOKE FAIRIES	YEAR SEVEN	3	1

12 ~ Running Up That Hill (A Deal With God)

UK: EMI KB1 (1985).
  B-side: *Under The Ivy*.

17.08.85: 9-4-3-5-8-15-23-33-49-61-75
19.05.12: 51
25.08.12: 6-33-63 (2012 Remix)
6.09.14: 51-98
9.06.22: 8-2-**1-1-1**-3-5-8-9-9-14-19-20-23-22-25-30-32-34-35-52-48-44-55-60-67-82-98-
  x-x-x-55-77-88-90-91-86

Pos	LW		Title, Artist		Peak Pos	WoC
1	2 ↑		**RUNNING UP THAT HILL** KATE BUSH	FISH PEOPLE	1	20
2	1 ↓		**AS IT WAS** HARRY STYLES	COLUMBIA	1	11
3	3		**GO** CAT BURNS	RCA/SINCE 93	2	22

Austria
1.11.85: 21-21-21 (bi-weekly)
7.06.22: 17-4-**3**-5-5-4-6-7-8-11-14-20-23-30-33-37-45-49-64-73

Australia
23.09.85: peaked at no.6, charted for 17 weeks
6.06.22: 2-**1-1**-2-**1-1-1-1-1-1-1**-2-6-7-10-13-17-20-29-32-38

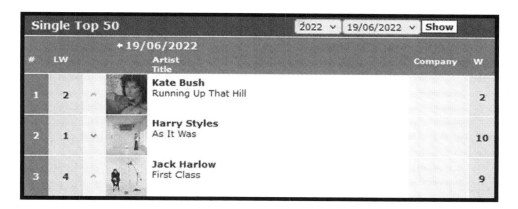

Belgium
31.08.85: 26-12-12-8-**6-6**-12-14-40
9.07.22: 33-35-41-x-45

Canada
7.09.85: 96-90-84-77-68-60-53-44-31-21-18-17-16-16-25-39-39-39-47-55-58-64-68-78
11.06.22: 4-**2-2**-7-4-3-3-3-5-6-9-13-17-19-18-25-30-35-39-44

Denmark
8.06.22: 24-**6**-9-13-18-12-8-10-13-17-27-30-36

Finland
09.85: 15 (monthly)
4.06.22: **6**-7-10-18-12-13-16-18-20

France
26.10.85: 43-38-34-27-25-27-24-29-35-32-40-28-31-36-38-x-49
18.08.12: 64 (2012 Remix)
3.06.22: 18-**3-3**-10-11-15-9-12-15-16-17-22-26-28-33-37-59-69-78-78-88-99

Germany
2.09.85: 63-22-13-4-**3-3-3-3**-4-6-12-16-19-30-36-46-56-62-63
3.06.22: 14-4-4-4-6-5-7-11-11-11-12-15-15-21-22-26-28-38-48-56-51-57-65-68-65-92
6.01.23: 82-80-84-100-93

Italy
2.06.22: 62-**18**-23-30-34-25-24-30-35-41-46-56-56-62-64-68-94-96

Ireland
25.08.85: 5-4-7-6-13
16.08.12: 22-30-80 (2012 Remix)
3.06.22: 10-3-**1-1-1-1-1-1-1-1**-2-17-20-20-22-27-29-30-31-36-39-45-50-47-65-82-89-99-
100

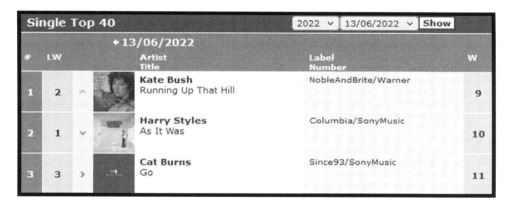

Pos	LW	Title, Artist			Peak Pos	WoC
1	3 ↑		**RUNNING UP THAT HILL** KATE BUSH	FISH PEOPLE	1	3
2	1 ↓		**AS IT WAS** HARRY STYLES	COLUMBIA	1	11
3	2 ↓		**ABOUT DAMN TIME** LIZZO	ATLANTIC	2	7

6.01.23: 71-85

New Zealand
27.10.85: 30-30-32-26-36-30-x-46
6.06.22: 2-**1-1**-2-2-2-2-2-4-7-9-11-15-19-20-26-33-37

Single Top 40				2022 ⌄	13/06/2022 ⌄	Show
⬇ 13/06/2022						
#	LW			Artist Title	Label Number	W
1	2	∧		**Kate Bush** Running Up That Hill	NobleAndBrite/Warner	9
2	1	∨		**Harry Styles** As It Was	Columbia/SonyMusic	10
3	3	>		**Cat Burns** Go	Since93/SonyMusic	11

Netherlands
24.08.85: 23-9-8-8-6-6-7-10-17-27-33-49
4.06.22: 26-**3**-4-8-7-6-9-12-15-20-25-41-44-52-67-69-74-82-96

Norway
28.05.22: 20-**4**-7-16-13-11-10-11-15-20-23-28-37

Spain
12.06.22: **48**-53-59-62-50-52-63-68-80-90

Sweden
3.06.22: 17-**1**-3-6-7-3-4-4-5-6-12-15-19-26-39-46-47-54-77-91

6.01.23: 71

Switzerland
29.09.85: 25-17-16-14-10-15-14-19-23-29-26
5.06.22: 4-**1**-2-2-3-2-3-4-5-9-10-14-20-24-29-33-34-38-44-53-66-73-85

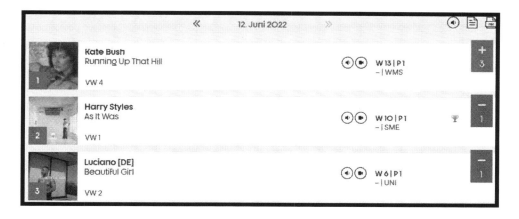

USA
7.09.85: 95-90-82-72-70-63-57-47-42-39-35-31-30-43-58-68-75-79-91-99
11.06.22: 8-4-5-9-6-4-4-**3-3**-4-4-5-4-4-9-12-19-26-31-45

Kate wrote and recorded *Running Up That Hill* for her fifth album, *HOUNDS OF LOVE*, released in 1985.

'*Running Up That Hill* was one of the first songs that I wrote for the album,' she said. 'It was very nice for me that it was the first single released, I'd always hoped that would be the way.'

The song itself is about a man and a woman who are deeply in love, but are also very insecure, and fear for the relationship itself.

'I had an idea of what I wanted to say in the song and I actually asked Del (Palmer) to write me a drum pattern,' said Kate, 'and he wrote this great pattern in the drum machine. So I just put the Fairlight on top of it and that was the basis of the song, with the drone, which played quite an important part.

'It's very much about two people who are in love, a man and a woman, and the idea of it is they could swap places ~ the man being the woman and vice versa, and they'd understand each other better. In some ways talking about the fundamental differences between men and women, I suppose trying to remove those obstacles, being in someone else's place, understanding how they see it, and hoping that would remove problems in the relationship.'

Running Up That Hill was originally titled *A Deal With God*, but EMI feared the word 'God' in the title might lead to a negative reaction. Kate, somewhat reluctantly, agreed to change the song's title to the more inoffensive *Running Up That Hill*.

EMI executives, initially, wanted to release *Cloudbusting* as the lead single from *HOUNDS OF LOVE*, but on this issue Kate refused to give in, and insisted *Running Up That Hill* be issued first ~ with hindsight, a wise decision.

Kate promoted *Running Up That Hill* with a music video directed by David Garfath, which featured a complicated dance routine with Kate dancing with Michael Hervieu, which was choreographed by Diane Grey.

'That was a lot of fun,' said Kate. 'I was working there with Diane Grey, a choreographer, who I met a couple of years ago. It's very exciting working with other people. I think it's especially so when you spend such a lot of time, say, in the studio where you're only working with a set group, say, two other people. And it was very inspiring working with the choreographer, who's also such a good dancer and we got on well together. We had lots of fun.'

Initially, rather than show the official music video, MTV chose to screen Kate's performance of *Running Up That Hill* on the popular BBC TV show *Wogan*, instead.

Running Up That Hill gave Kate a Top 3 hit in Germany and the UK, and achieved no.4 in Ireland, no.6 in Australia, Belgium and the Netherlands, no.10 in Switzerland, no.15 in Finland, no.16 in Canada, no.21 in Austria, no.24 in France, no.26 in New Zealand and no.30 in the United States.

'I am very excited about how it's been received by people!' enthused Kate. 'It's so rewarding after working for a long time to see that your work is being received with open arms.'

Running Up That Hill, with its original title *Running Up That Hill (A Deal With God)* restored, was reissued in 2012. Although the release was labelled as the '2012 Remix', it wasn't actually a remix at all, as Kate recorded new vocals over the extended backing track of the extended 12" single released in 1985. This up-dated version premiered during the closing ceremony of the 2012 Summer Olympic Games, staged in London, although Kate herself didn't appear. The up-dated recording also featured on the compilation album, *A SYMPHONY OF BRITISH MUSIC*, which was sub-titled 'Music for the Closing Ceremony of the London 2012 Olympic Games'.

The up-dated version returned *Running Up That Hill (A Deal With God)* to the Top 10 in the UK, where it peaked at no.6. The 2012 version also achieved no.22 in Ireland, and was a minor no.64 hit in France.

In 2022, *Running Up That Hill (A Deal With God)* was used in Series 4 of the Netflix TV show, *Stranger Things*. As a result, the popularity of the song soared, and it re-entered the chart in numerous countries, and achieved a new peak position in many.

'It's hard to take in the speed at which this has all been happening,' said Kate. 'So many young people who love the show are discovering the song for the first time … We've all been astounded to watch the track explode!'

In the UK, *Running Up That Hill (A Deal With God)* hit no.1 for three weeks, giving Kate only her second chart topping single, following her debut, *Wuthering Heights*. In doing so, Kate set three new chart records:

- Longest gap between no.1 singles ~ 44 years
- Longest time taken for a single to reach no.1 ~ 37 years
- Oldest woman to have a no.1 single ~ age 63 years

Running Up That Hill (A Deal With God) also hit no.1 in Australia, Ireland, New Zealand, Sweden and Switzerland, and charted at no.2 in Canada, no.3 in Austria, France, the Netherlands and the United States, no.4 in Germany and Norway, no.6 in Denmark and Finland, no.18 in Italy, no.33 in Belgium and no.48 in Spain.

INTERNATIONAL
musician
AND RECORDING WORLD

INCORPORATING ELECTRONIC SOUNDMAKER & COMPUTER MUSIC / WHAT KEYBOARD?

OCTOBER 1985
£1.50
DM11

KATE BUSH
Back In The Running

NEW ORDER
TONY THOMPSON
HUGH CORNWELL
SIMPLY RED
SHRIEKBACK
CHRISSIE HYNDE/UB40

TESTS
Fender guitars
E-Mu SP-12 drum machine
Yamaha Rev 7 reverb
Trak 205 deep shell kit
Bit 99 synth
Roland SRV2000 reverb
MDB Window Recorder sampler
MPC Mark 2 electronic kit
Seymour Duncan pickups

Best Of The West: British Music Fair Reviewed
Secrets Of The East: Ethnic Instruments Revealed

WIN
A Mesa Boogie amp
worth £1275

How To Write Lyrics
Winning The War Of The Words

13 ~ Cloudbusting

UK: EMI KB2 (1985).
  B-side: *Burning Bridge*.

26.10.85: 26-**20-20**-27-43-60-x-87-95

Belgium
16.11.85: 38-**16**-23-26-28-33

Germany
25.11.85: 73-35-23-**20-20**-22-21-29-35-49-61-71

Ireland
3.11.85: 17-**13**-21-30

Netherlands
23.11.85: 16-14-**13**-14-16-23-34-36

Kate wrote and recorded *Cloudbusting* for her *HOUNDS OF LOVE* album.
    'This was inspired by a book that I first found on a shelf nearly nine years ago,' said Kate. 'It was just calling me from the shelf, and when I read it I was very moved by the magic of it. It's about a special relationship between a young son and his father. The book was written from a child's point of view. His father is everything to him; he is the magic in his life, and he teaches him everything, teaching him to be open-minded and not to build up barriers. His father has built a machine that can make it rain, a 'cloudbuster', and

the son and his father go out together cloudbusting. They point big pipes up into the sky, and they make it rain.'

The book in question was Peter Reich's 1973 publication, *A Book Of Dreams*, which was a memoir of his father, Wilhelm Reich.

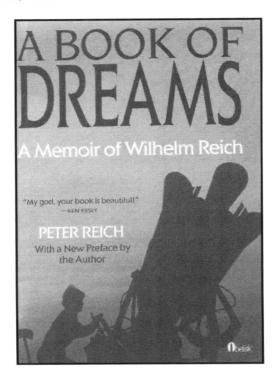

In the accompanying music video, directed by Julian Doyle, Kate played the part of Peter Reich, with actor Donald Sutherland as Peter's father, Wilhelm. Around the time *Cloudbusting* was released, Kate sent the real Peter Wilhelm a copy of the music video.

'These were worrying moments for me,' she admitted. 'What if he didn't like it? If I'd got it wrong? But he said he found them very emotional and that I'd captured the situation. This was the ultimate reward for me.'

'Quite magically,' said Peter Reich, 'this British musician had tapped precisely into a unique and magical fulfilment of father-son devotion, emotion and understanding. They had captured it all.'

Although it wasn't as successful as *Running Up That Hill*, *Cloudbusting* charted at no.13 in Ireland and the Netherlands, no.16 in Belgium, and no.20 in Germany and the UK.

In 2019, *Cloudbusting* was reissued as a limited edition 12" picture disc featuring four tracks:

- *Cloudbusting (The Orgonon Mix)*
- *Under The Ivy*

- *Rocket Man*
- *Warm And Soothing*

Although *Cloudbusting* failed to re-enter any mainstream charts, it did go to no.1 for two weeks on the Official Chart Company's Vinyl Singles chart in the UK.

Pos	LW	Title, Artist			Peak Pos	WoC
1	New		**CLOUDBUSTING** KATE BUSH	FISH PEOPLE	1	1
2	1 ↓		**BOYS KEEP SWINGING** DAVID BOWIE	PARLOPHONE	1	2
3	5 ↑		**WEDDING BELL BLUES** MORRISSEY	BMG	1	4

14 ~ Hounds Of Love

UK: KB3 (1986).
  B-side: *The Handsome Cabin Boy.*

1.03.86: 26-**18**-24-38-58

Canada
8.03.86: 91-86-**84-84**-96

Germany
14.04.86: **68**-x-70

Ireland
9.03.86: **12-12**-29

Kate wrote and recorded *Hounds Of Love* for her album with the same title.

 'The ideas for *Hounds Of Love*, the title track,' said Kate, 'are very much to do with love itself and people being afraid of it, the idea of wanting to run away from love, not to let love catch them, and trap them, in case the hounds might want to tear them to pieces, and it's very much using the imagery of love as something coming to get you and you've got to run away from it or you won't survive.'

 Kate wrote *Hounds Of Love*, as she did with many of her songs, at home, and it was one of the earliest songs she wrote for her fifth album.

 'It was inspired in some ways by this old black and white movie that is a real favorite of ours,' she said, 'called *Night Of The Demon*. It's all about this demon that appears in the trees, and the line at the top of the song, "It's in the trees, it's coming…" is actually taken from the film. Maurice Denham is the guy that sang it.'

Hounds Of Love was chosen as the third single from Kate's *HOUNDS OF LOVE* album, but she found both the 12" single and the music video a challenge.

'The twelve-inch of *Hounds Of Love* has been the most demanding so far,' she revealed. 'It's a short song, with very little tuned instrumentation, so we decided to go for an alternative lead vocal over the existing track, with a few changes here and there ~ it seemed an interesting solution. Del (Palmer) and I re-did the vocal, the B-side and the mixes in two days ~ that's some kind of record for me!'

Kate found following the *Cloudbusting* music video 'extremely difficult'.

'I still wanted to follow the approach of making a short film,' she said, 'and this time we wanted to suggest a piece of (Alfred) Hitchcock: a short thriller. Paddy (Kate's brother) inspired me into a 39 Steps theme, and for the two-three weeks over Christmas my life became this third video.'

The B-side of *Hounds Of Love*, unusually, wasn't one of Kate's own compositions. *The Handsome Cabin Boy* is a traditional folk song also known as *The Female Cabin Boy*, and dates back to at least 1905.

Hounds Of Love achieved no.12 in Ireland and no.18 in the UK, and was a minor hit in Canada and Germany.

In 2004, the English band The Futureheads recorded a cover of *Hounds Of Love* which, when released as a single, charted at no.8 in the UK and no.26 in Ireland.

15 ~ The Big Sky

Kate Bush ~ The Big Sky
(Special Single Mix)

UK: EMI KB4 (1986).
  B-side: *Not This Time*.

10.05.86: 39-**37**-54-x-84-84

Ireland
25.05.86: 16-**15**

Kate wrote and recorded *The Big Sky* for her *HOUNDS OF LOVE* album.

'*Big Sky* was a song that changed a lot between the first version of it on the demo and the end product on the master tapes,' said Kate. 'The demos are the masters, in that we now work straight in the 24-track studio when I'm writing the songs; but the structure of this song changed quite a lot. I wanted to steam along, and with the help of musicians such as Alan Murphy on guitar and Youth on bass, we accomplished quite a rock-and-roll feel for the track.'

Kate's inspiration for the song, as the title suggests, was the sky.

'Someone sitting looking at the sky,' she said, 'watching the clouds change. I used to do this a lot as a child, just watching the clouds go into different shapes. I think we forget these pleasures as adults. We don't get as much time to enjoy those kinds of things, or think about them, we feel silly about what we used to do naturally. The song is also suggesting the coming of the next flood ~ how perhaps the fools on the hills will be the wise ones.'

The Big Sky, Kate readily admitted, was a difficult song to write.

'I knew what I wanted to finish up with,' she said, 'but I didn't seem to be able to get there! We had three different versions and eventually it just kind of turned into what it did, thank goodness.'

The Big Sky was issued as the fourth and final single from *HOUNDS OF LOVE*. A 'Special Single Mix' was released, and Kate directed the accompanying music video herself, which was later nominated for Best Female Video at the MTV Video Music Awards.

The Big Sky was issued as a 7" picture disc single in the UK.

The Big Sky charted at no.15 in Ireland and no.37 in the UK, but it wasn't a hit anywhere else.

16 ~ Don't Give Up

UK: Virgin PGS2 (1986).
  B-side: *In Your Eyes (Special Mix)* (Peter Gabriel).

1.11.86: 31-16-**9**-**9**-12-24-36-48-55-49-62

Australia
16.02.87: peaked at no.**5**, charted for 23 weeks

Belgium
3.01.87: 13-12-**9**-**9**-11-11-23

Canada
18.04.87: 98-82-76-61-53-51-49-43-**40**-48-49-56-72

Germany
17.11.86: 57-53-35-**27**-30-34-41-55-58-57-74

Ireland
2.11.86: 15-**4**-5-11-20

Netherlands
22.11.86: 34-20-15-13-10-**5**-7-10-15-28-36-48-58-73-73-83

New Zealand
22.02.87: 43-34-23-**16**-21-17-**16**-25-20-31-28-34-36-50

Don't Give Up was composed by Peter Gabriel, and he recorded the song as a duet with Kate for his 1986 album, *SO*.

'Kate did a great job,' said Peter Gabriel. 'I'm a great fan of her singing and her voice. I think she sang that track differently to how she sings on her own records, in a very sensitive way. There are similarities in the way we work. She works as slowly as I do, which is reassuring.'

Don't Give Up was the third single released from *SO*, and was promoted with two different music videos. The first, directed by Godley & Creme, had Kate and Peter Gabriel embracing and singing, while the sun behind them enters a total eclipse, and then re-emerges. On filming the promo, Peter Gabriel quipped, 'There are worse ways to earn a living!'

The second music video, which was less commonly screened, was directed by Jim Blashfield, and featured Kate's and Peter Gabriel's faces superimposed over footage of a town and its people in total disrepair.

Don't Give Up was Kate's third collaboration with Peter Gabriel, but it was the first where she was actually credited on the record. The single achieved no.4 in Ireland, no.5 in Australia and the Netherlands, no.9 in Belgium and the UK, no.16 in New Zealand, no.27 in Germany and no.40 in Canada. The single was also a minor no.72 hit on the Hot 100 in the United States.

There have been a number of cover versions of *Don't Give Up* over the years, including:

- Willie Nelson & Sinéad O'Connor
- Alicia Keys & Bono
- Shannon Noll & Natalie Bassingthwaighte

Alicia Keys & Bono's cover of *Don't Give Up* was a minor no.79 hit on the Hot 100 in the United States in 2005, while Shannon Noll & Natalie Bassingthwaighte took the song to no.2 in their native Australia the following year.

17 ~ Experiment IV

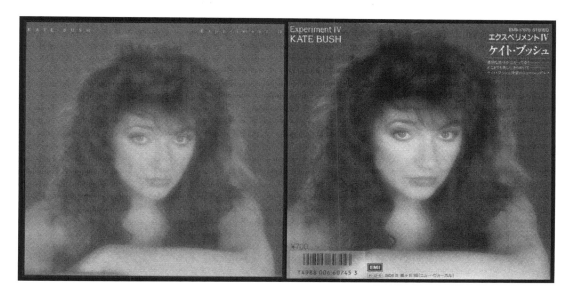

UK: EMI KB5 (1986).
  B-side: *Wuthering Heights (New Vocal).*

8.11.86: 40-**23**-35-54

Germany
8.12.86: 55-55-**50**-54-63-64-72

Ireland
9.11.86: 18-**12**-19

Kate wrote and recorded *Experiment IV* for her first compilation album, *THE WHOLE STORY*, released in 1986.

According to Kate, the song is about 'a nightmare vision of the future where music is harnessed by evil scientists as a weapon of destruction.'

'I don't think it's always what I think about scientists,' she said, 'but I think they are fascinating in that so often they're trying to create something that they consider positive, productive and very much something that would help mankind, but so often along the way those good intentions end up being used, particularly by other people, for completely the opposite reasons. Particularly experiments that end up being used by the military, things like the atom bomb. I can see that perhaps when the guy was originally playing with that idea, he had no idea where he'd end up, and that I'm sure that he wouldn't have the evil intentions in his head initially. He was so caught up, so obsessed with the pure level of the science that he didn't actually realise how it could be used.'

Experiment IV featured Nigel Kennedy on violin, and at one point during the song he replicated the screeching violins heard in the famous shower scene in Alfred Hitchcock's classic 1960 horror film, *Psycho*.

Kate explored the song's theme further in the accompanying music video, which she directed herself.

'Directing is a new experiment for me,' she said, 'actually, it was Experiment III ~ and with this track I had such strong visual ideas while I was writing the song that I wanted to give it another go. It's the first time the video and song have come together. It was very hard work, but a lot of fun.'

Kate filmed the promo in an old, disused hospital, where it was very cold and damp. The large cast included Dawn French, Hugh Laurie, Richard Vernon and Peter Vaughan, and Kate's brother Paddy played the lunatic.

'There were some wonderful moments,' said Kate, 'like filming in East London. We had a field full of dead bodies who kept moving about to get more comfortable, so we had to shout out over a loud-hailer, "Stop moving ~ you're supposed to be dead!" And the music shop that we created for the shot was so realistic that passers-by kept popping in wanting to buy some of the instruments.'

Surprising no one, the music video was banned by the BBC, as it was considered 'too violent' to be shown before the 9.00pm watershed. This meant, of course, the promo couldn't be shown on *Top Of The Pops* and other prime-time TV shows, which certainly adversely affected sales of *Experiment IV*, which nevertheless charted at no.12 in Ireland, no.23 in the UK and no.50 in Germany.

The B-side of *Experiment IV* was a newly recorded version of Kate's debut hit, *Wuthering Heights*, which also featured on her *THE WHOLE STORY* album.

Let It Be

UK: The Sun AID 1 (1987).
   B-side: *Let It Be (The Gospel Jam Mix)*.

4.04.87: **1-1-1**-4-17-34-58

Pos	LW	Title, Artist			Peak Pos	WoC
1	New	LET IT BE	**LET IT BE** FERRY AID	THE SUN	1	1
2	1 ↓		**RESPECTABLE** MEL AND KIM	SUPREME	1	5
3	9 ↑		**LET'S WAIT A WHILE** JANET JACKSON	BREAKOUT	3	3

Austria
15.05.87: 10-**4**-9-16-20-22-25 (bi-weekly)

Belgium
18.04.87: 18-8-**3**-4-6-8-12-24-38

France
25.04.87: 35-37-32-23-19-14-**8**-11-13-13-19-20-24-34-34

Germany
20.04.87: 47-8-5-4-4-**3**-7-9-12-14-29-39-47-63

Ireland
29.03.87: 22-**2-2**-3-7-21

Netherlands
11.04.87: 21-7-**4-4-4**-7-7-11-20-45-46-49-88

New Zealand
7.06.87: 22-16-11-**4**-11-23-38-47

Norway
18.04.87: 4-4-**1-1-1-1**-2-2-2-5-6

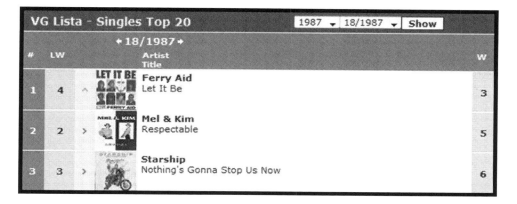

Sweden
6.05.87: 10-**9-9**-16-18

Switzerland
26.04.87: 3-**1-1-1-1**-2-**1**-3-3-8-11-11-25-19

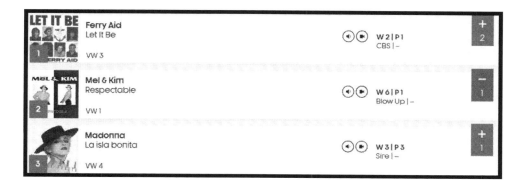

Let It Be was written by John Lennon & Paul McCartney, and was originally recorded by The Beatles for their 1970 album with the same title. The Beatles took the song to no.1 in Australia, Austria, Canada, The Netherlands, New Zealand, Norway, Switzerland and the United States, no.2 in Germany and the UK, and no.3 in Belgium and Ireland.

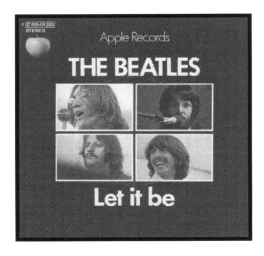

On 6th March 1987, in the Belgium port of Zeebrugge, the ferry *MS Herald of Free Enterprise* capsized and sank, with the loss of 193 passengers and crew. In response to the Zeebrugge Disaster Garry Bushell, who worked for *The Sun* newspaper at the time, organised a charity recording of *Let It Be*, which took place between the 15th and 17th March. The recording was credited to Ferry Aid.

Kate was one of the numerous artists who contributed to the recording. Other soloists on the recording included Paul McCartney, Andy Bell, Boy George, Edwin Starr, Jackie Graham, Kim Wilde, Mel and Kim, Nik Kershaw, Pepsi & Shirley and Ruby Turner. Gary Moore and Mark Knopfler performed the guitar solo.

The chorus featured a host of other artists, including Alvin Stardust, Bananarama, Bonnie Tyler, Bucks Fizz, The Drifters, Errol Brown, Frankie Goes To Hollywood, Go West, Hazel Dean, Imagination, Loose Ends, Maxi Priest, New Seekers, The Nolans and Suzi Quatro.

Ferry Aid's cover of *Let It Be* topped the charts in Norway, Switzerland and the UK, and achieved no.2 in Ireland, no.3 in Belgium and Germany, no.4 in Austria, the Netherlands and New Zealand, no.8 in France and no.9 in Sweden.

18 ~ The Sensual World

UK: EMI EM 102 (1989).
  B-side: *Walk Straight Down The Middle.*

30.09.89: **12**-15-29-44-65

Australia
5.11.89: 45-x-**44-44**

Belgium
14.10.89: 49-37-**31**-36-38-33-43

Canada
4.11.89: 81-74-66-60-**58**-64-65-98

Germany
16.10.89: 78-69-**29**-33-36-40-48-65-73-85-83-86-87-91

Ireland
24.09.89: 30-**6**-9

Italy
14.10.89: peaked at no.**16**, charted for 8 weeks

Netherlands
30.09.89: 76-45-29-22-**20**-24-33-53-73-94

4 FREE POSTCARDS inside *

7 October 1989   55p

EMILY LLOYD ★ THE THE
GEORGE CLINTON ★ EPMD

NEW MUSICAL EXPRESS
NME

Better Kate than never

THE CLASH
A classic interview revisited

THE
WONDER
STUFF
Hup
and
away

KATE BUSH
Talks Sensual

* Postcards not available in some overseas countries

Kate Bush pictured by Kevin Cummins

Kate wrote and recorded *The Sensual World* for her sixth studio album, also titled *THE SENSUAL WORLD*, which was released in 1989. Originally, Kate wanted to set to music the words spoken by the character Molly Bloom, at the end of the James Joyce novel, *Ulysses*.

'We couldn't get permission to use the words,' said Kate. 'I tried for a long time ~ probably about a year ~ and they (the James Joyce estate) wouldn't let me use them, so I had to create something that sounded like those original words, had the same rhythm, the same kind of feel, but obviously not being able to use them. It all kind of turned in to a pastiche of it and that's why the book character, Molly Bloom, then steps out into the real world and becomes one of us.'

The song is about someone from a book who steps out from this very black and white 2-D world into the real world.

'The immediate impressions was the sensuality of this world,' said Kate, 'the fact that you can touch things, that is so sensual, you know ... the colours of trees, the feel of the grass on the feet, the touch of this in the hand ~ the fact that it is such a sensual world. I think for me that's an incredibly important thing about this planet, that we are surrounded by such sensuality and yet we tend not to see it like that. But I'm sure for someone who had never experienced it before it would be quite a devastating thing.'

In the accompanying music video, which Kate and Peter Richardson directed, Kate is seen wearing a medieval dress, as she dances through an enchanted forest.

'It's really conveying what I feel about *The Sensual World*,' she said, 'which is that it's an incredible planet that we live in. It has tremendous sensuality, the texture and the colours of everything that nature supplies is incredibly beautiful.'

The Sensual World was released as the lead single from the album with the same title, and achieved no.6 in Ireland, no.12 in the UK, no.16 in Italy, no.20 in the Netherlands, no.29 in Germany, no.31 in Belgium, no.44 in Australia and no.58 in Canada.

More than twenty years after she recorded *The Sensual World*, Kate re-recorded the song as she had originally intended, using the character Molly Bloom's closing words from *Ulysses*, for her 2011 album, *DIRECTOR'S CUT* ~ the song was re-titled *Flower Of The Mountain*.

19 ~ This Woman's Work

UK: EMI EM 119 (1989).
  B-side: *Be Kind To My Mistakes*.

2.12.89: 30-**25**-31-41-45
12.01.08: 76
6.09.14: 80

Ireland
3.12.89: **20**-25

Kate was asked to write the song that became *This Woman's Work* for the 1988 movie, *She's Having A Baby*.

'John Hughes, the director, rung up and said that he had a sequence in the film that he really wanted a song written to be with,' said Kate. 'When he sent the piece of film that the song was going to be (part of), I just thought it was wonderful, it was so moving, a very moving piece of film. And in a way, there was a sense that the whole film built up to this moment … it was a very easy song to write. It was very quick, and just kind of came, like a lot of songs do. Even if you struggle for months, in the end, they just kind of go ~ BLAH!'

In the film, *This Woman's Work* played over the dramatic climax, when the character Jake, played by actor Kevin Bacon, learns that the lives of his wife Kirsty (Elizabeth McGovern) and their unborn child are in danger ~ the scene features a montage of flashbacks to happier times.

This Woman's Work originally featured on the accompanying soundtrack album, released in 1988.

Kate was in two minds about whether or not to include *This Woman's Work* to her new album, *THE SENSUAL WORLD*.

'I must say that Del (Palmer) was very instrumental in saying that I should put it on the album,' she admitted, 'and I'm very glad I did because I had the most fantastic response ~ in some ways, maybe the greatest response ~ to this song. And I was really ~ I was absolutely thrilled.'

Kate re-edited *This Woman's Work*, for her own album, and a third edit was released as the second single from *THE SENSUAL WORLD*.

Kate directed the music video for *This Woman's Work* herself.

'It was interesting because the song had originally been written to visuals,' she observed, 'but the song has its own storyline as well, so then it was like making a film of the song. Obviously (in the movie) it's about a man waiting for his wife having a baby.

Now I didn't want to put myself in a situation where I have to be pregnant! It's all too complicated, so left it very ambiguous, and I think it looks like a little film in that it tells a story.'

In the promo, Kate played the wife/girlfriend herself, while her distraught partner was played by Tim McInnemy.

'Tim is kind of sitting throughout the song,' Kate explained, 'waiting for his girlfriend or whoever who's in the hospital, so most of the video is very distressed. You know, he's in a real distressed state and he sort of looks up, and then the light goes away from the window, this spot comes down. So he's just sitting in this spot and he's like, he's suddenly conjuring up these memories, and then I sort of step in with a raincoat and put it 'round his shoulders.'

As the second single from *THE SENSUAL WORLD*, *This Woman's Work* achieved no.20 in Ireland and no.25 in the UK, but it wasn't a hit anywhere else.

In the UK, *This Woman's Work* was issued as a limited edition 7" picture disc single.

Kate re-recorded *This Woman's Work* for her 2011 album, *DIRECTOR'S CUT* ~ this was a simpler, stripped down version, featuring Kate singing and playing the piano.

In 2012, the American R&B singer Maxwell's MTV Unplugged cover of *This Woman's Work* was promoted as a single, and charted at no.41 in the UK and no.58 on the Hot 100 in the United States.

20 ~ Love And Anger

UK: EMI EM 134 (1990).
  B-side: *Ken (From The Comic Strip Film G.L.C.).*

10.03.90: 39-**38**-69

Kate wrote and recorded *Love And Anger* for her *THE SENSUAL WORLD* album ~ the track featured Pink Floyd's David Gilmour on guitar. It was a song that took Kate more than eighteen months to write.

'I just couldn't get any lyrics or work out what to do with the instruments,' she explained. 'I just didn't know what I wanted to say … If I'm saying anything, it's that if people are having a hard time and things look really dark, and it seems like you can't get out, then try not to worry too much. It'll be all right ~ someone will come and help.'

Released as the third and final single from the album, *Love And Anger* made its chart debut at no.39 in the UK, and climbed one place in its second week, before falling out of the Top 40. The single failed to enter any other mainstream charts, but *Love And Anger* did go all the way to no.1 on Billboard's Alternative Airplay (Modern Rock Tracks) chart in the United States ~ it was Kate's first and only chart topping release on any of Billboard's numerous charts.

Kate wrote the B-side of *Love And Anger*, *Ken*, for the 'GLC: The Carnage Continues…' episode of the British TV show, *The Comic Strip. Ken* was used as the theme song for a parody of a Hollywood blockbuster about the British politician, Ken Livingstone.

21 ~ Rocket Man

UK: Mercury TRIBO 2 (1991).
  B-side: *Candle In The Wind (Vocal Version)*.

7.12.91: 13-**12**-18-19-23-43-74-70

Australia
26.01.92: 49-28-27-25-23-14-12-5-**2**-8-14-21-28-46

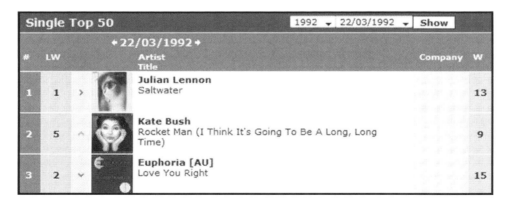

France
25.01.92: 50-50-**45**-47-47-47

Germany
3.02.92: 96-90-**36**-37-**36**-39-50-88-92

Ireland
8.12.91: **20**-23

Netherlands
14.12.91: 92-81-61-41-30-**27**-32-52-74

Switzerland
19.01.92: 23-28-22-**20**-28-32 (bi-weekly)

Rocket Man, or *Rocket Man (It's Going To Be A Long, Long Time)* as the song is officially known, was written by Elton John and Bernie Taupin, and was originally recorded by Elton for his 1972 album, *HONKY CHATEAU*. As a single, *Rocket Man* charted at no.2 in the UK, no.6 in Ireland and the United States, no.8 in Canada, no.11 in New Zealand, no.13 in Australia and no.18 in Germany.

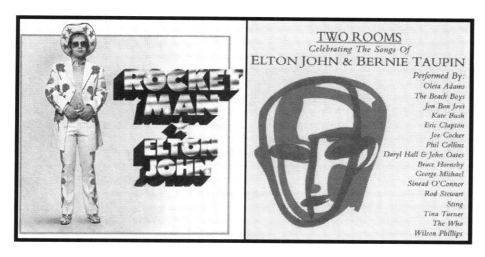

A big Elton John fan since childhood, Kate was thrilled when she was approached, and asked if she wanted to record a cover of one of Elton's songs for a tribute Elton John/Bernie Taupin album, *TWO ROOMS*.

'I was really knocked out to be asked to be involved with this project,' she said, 'because I was such a big fan of Elton's when I was little. I really loved his stuff. It's like he's my biggest hero, really, and when I was just starting to write songs he was the only songwriter I knew of that played the piano and sang and wrote songs.'

Rocket Man was Kate's favourite Elton John song.

'They basically said, "Would we like to be involved?",' she said. 'I could choose which track I wanted … *Rocket Man* was my favourite and I hoped it hadn't gone, actually ~ I hoped no one else was going to do it.'

Luckily for Kate, no one else involved with the project had chosen *Rocket Man*.

'I actually haven't heard the original for a very long time ~ a long, long time!,' she said, laughing. 'It was just that I wanted to do it differently. I do think that if you cover records, you should try and make them different. It's like remaking movies: you've got to try and give it something that makes it worth re-releasing, and the reggae treatment just seemed to happen, really. I just tried to put the chords together on the piano, and it just seemed to want to take off in the choruses. So we gave it the reggae treatment.'

TWO ROOMS, sub-titled 'Celebrating the Songs of Elton John & Bernie Taupin', was released in 1991, and rose to no.18 on the Billboard 200 in the United States.

No one was more surprised than Kate, when more than two years later she learned of plans to release her cover of *Rocket Man* as a single.

'We were quite astounded when they wanted to release it as a single just recently' she admitted. 'What's very nice is that the guitarist that played on the track, Alan Murphy, who was our guitarist at the time, died not long after the track was made. So this was one of the last things that he did with us, and it's particularly nice for me to feel that it's not only keeping him alive, but I know that he would be really thrilled to know it was doing so well, and it's nice for all of us that loved Al to know that he can be a part of this now.'

For the B-side of *Rocket Man*, Kate recorded a cover of Elton John's tribute to Marilyn Monroe, *Candle In The Wind*, which was a hit in 1973.

Kate took *Rocket Man* to no.2 in Australia, no.12 in the UK, no.20 in Ireland and Switzerland, no.27 in the Netherlands, no.36 in Germany and no.45 in France.

22 ~ Rubberband Girl

UK: EMI EM 280 (1993).
  B-side: *Big Stripey Lie*.

18.09.93: **12**-14-36-50-60

Australia
24.10.93: 48-42-42-**39**-48

Belgium
9.10.93: **47**

Canada
16.10.93: 94-65-**50-50**-82-92
24.01.94: 79-72-92-100

Germany
25.10.93: 68-81-**65**-72-72-74-71-94

Ireland
12.09.93: 21-**17**-20

Italy
2.10.93: peaked at no.**22**, charted for 2 weeks

Netherlands
2.10.93: 42-**37**-42

New Zealand
17.10.93: 39-x-**34**-50-48

USA
25.12.93: **88**-99-97-95-93-99

Kate wrote and recorded *Rubberband Girl* for her seventh studio album, *THE RED SHOES*, which was released in 1993.

'On *Rubberband Girl* the bass, drums and basic keyboards were all done together,' said Del Palmer. 'We did change the whole track afterwards in the sense of editing it digitally rather than re-doing tracks. The bass and drum sound was important because we wanted to have them consistent throughout the album.'

Rubberband Girl was chosen as the lead single from *THE RED SHOES* in most countries, however, in North America the Caribbean-tinged *Eat The Music* was preferred. Kate promoted the release of *Rubberband Girl* with a highly choreographed music video, largely filmed with a line of male musicians as the backdrop.

Rubberband Girl achieved no.12 in the UK, no.17 in Ireland, no.22 in Italy, no.34 in New Zealand, no.37 in the Netherlands, no.39 in Australia, no.47 in Belgium and no.50 in Canada. The single was also a minor hit in Germany and the United States.

Rubberband Girl was issued as a 12" picture disc single in the UK.

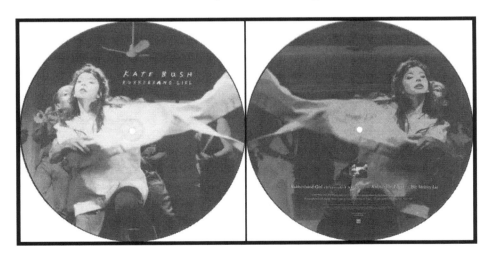

Kate re-recorded *Rubberband Girl* for her 2011 album, *DIRECTOR'S CUT*.

23 ~ Moments Of Pleasure

UK: EMI CDEM 297 (1993).
 Tracks: *Show A Little Devotion/December Will Be Magic Again/Experiment IV*.

27.11.93: **26**-32-51

Kate wrote and recorded the ballad *Moments Of Pleasure* for her *THE RED SHOES* album, and in the song she remembered friends and family who were no longer with us, including Michael Powell, who directed the 1948 film, *The Red Shoes*, and who Kate had met in New York not long before he passed away.

 'I'd had a few conversations with him and I'd been dying to meet him,' said Kate. 'As we came out of the lift, he was standing outside with his walking stick, and he was pretending to be someone like Douglas Fairbanks. He was completely adorable, and just the most beautiful spirit, and it was a very profound experience for me.'

 Moments Of Pleasure also remembered Alan Murphy (*aka* Smurf), Bill Duffield, Gary Hurst, John Barrett and Kate's aunt, Maureen. Kate's mother Hannah, who was ill at the time, was also mentioned; sadly, she passed away shortly after the song was recorded.

 In most countries, *Moments Of Pleasure* was released as the second single from *THE RED SHOES*. The single entered the UK chart at no.26, but it only managed three weeks on the Top 100, and it wasn't a hit anywhere else.

 Kate re-recorded *Moments Of Pleasure* for her 2011 album, *DIRECTOR'S CUT*.

24 ~ The Red Shoes

UK: EMI CDEMS 316 (1994).
   Tracks: *You Want Alchemy/Cloudbusting (Video Mix)/This Woman's Work.*

16.04.94: 28-**21**-53-77

Kate wrote and recorded *The Red Shoes* for her album with the same title.
   The song was inspired by a character in the 1948 film, *The Red Shoes*, a girl who puts on a pair of enchanted red ballet slippers, and can't stop dancing until she breaks the spell. The backing vocalists on the recording included Kate's brother, Paddy.
   Kate explored the song's theme further in the music video, which she filmed to promote the release of *The Red Shoes* as a single. Like *Moments Of Please* before it, *The Red Shoes* was only a hit in one country ~ it entered the UK singles chart at no.28, and peaked at no.21 the following week.
   Two CD singles were released, with the second featuring a 10 minute remix of *The Red Shoes*, re-titled *Shoedance*. The CD also featured remixes of *The Big Sky* and *Running Up That Hill.*

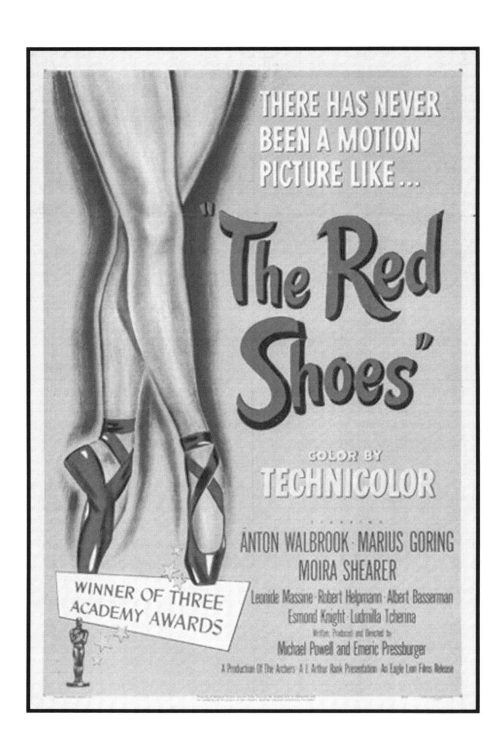

25 ~ The Man I Love

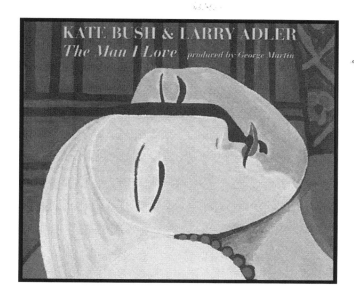

UK: Mercury MERCD 408 (1994).
   Tracks: *Rhapsody In Blue/(Edit)* (Larry Adler & George Martin).

30.07.94: **27**-56-88-95

The Man I Love was written by George & Ira Gershwin, for the score of the 1924 musical comedy, *Lady, Be Good* ~ however, the song was deleted from the show. *The Man I Love* was published three years later, when it did feature in another Gershwin show, the government satire, *Strike Up The Band*.

A number of popular recordings of *The Man I Love* appeared in 1928, including versions by Fred Rich & His Orchestra, Marion Harris, Paul Whiteman & His Orchestra and Sophie Tucker ~ the vocalist on both Orchestra recordings was Vaughn De Leath.

Kate recorded a cover of *The Man I Love* with the American harmonica player Larry Adler, for the 1994 George Gershwin tribute album, *THE GLORY OF GERSHWIN*. The album was produced by George Martin, who most famously worked with The Beatles.

Kate and Larry Adler filmed a simple, yet highly effective black/white music video, to promote the release of *The Man I Love* as a single. The single made its chart debut at no.27 in the UK, but it rose no higher, and it wasn't a hit anywhere else.

26 ~ And So Is Love

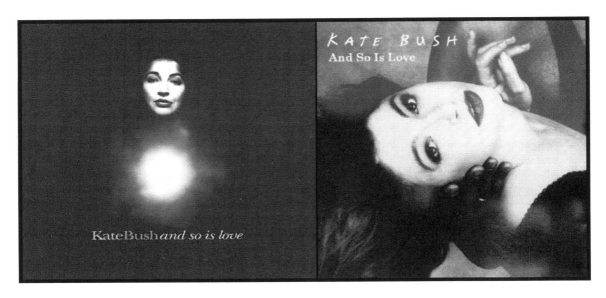

UK: EMI CDEM 355 (1994).
    Tracks: *Rubberband Girl (U.S. Mix)/Eat The Music (U.S. Mix)*.

19.11.94: **26**-51-86

Kate wrote and recorded *And So Is Love* for her *THE RED SHOES* album.
    The recording featured Eric Clapton on guitar and Procol Harum's Gary Brooker on Hammond organ. Eric Clapton recorded his contribution just two months after he lost his young son Conor, who had fallen 53 floors from a New York apartment window.
    'I admired him for doing that,' said Del Palmer. 'He'd promised to do it and he wanted to stick to his commitment.'
    And So Is Love was the final single released from *THE RED SHOES*, and like its predecessors it only charted in the UK, where it made its debut at no.26 before falling off the Top 100 after just three weeks.
    Kate re-recorded *And So Is Love*, with new lyrics, for her 2011 album, *DIRECTOR'S CUT*.

27 ~ King Of The Mountain

UK: EMI CDEM 674 (2005).
 Tracks: *Sexual Healing*.

5.11.05: **4**-8-21-31-53-66-96

Austria
6.11.05: **71**-72

Finland
5.11.05: **3**-5-15

#	LW			Artist Title		Label	W
				Singles Top 20	2005 ▾ 44/2005 ▾	Show	
				‹ **44/2005** ›			
1	1	›		**Nightwish** Sleeping Sun 2005		SPINEFARM	2
2	NEW	∧		**The Rasmus** Sail Away		PLAYGROUND	1
3	NEW	∧		**Kate Bush** King Of The Mountain		EMI	1

Germany
4.11.05: **42**-49-51-66-74-97

Ireland
27.10.05: peaked at no.**13**, charted for 2 weeks

Italy
27.10.05: peaked at no.**24**, charted for 3 weeks

Netherlands
29.10.05: 85-**13**-32-51-88

Switzerland
6.11.05: **47-47**-70-69-91

King Of The Mountain was a song Kate wrote way back in 1996 ~ the song mentions the late Elvis Presley, and gives a nod to the 1941 Orson Welles film, *Citizen Kane*.

'I don't think human beings are really built to withstand that kind of fame,' said Kate, referring to Elvis and his demise. She joked her unusual vocal delivery on *King Of The Mountain* was her impersonation of Elvis.

There was much speculation, throughout 2005, about a possible new Kate Bush album ~ what would be her first for 12 years. Finally, in early October, *King Of The Mountain* was issued as a single, with its parent album *AERIAL* released the following month.

Kate promoted *King Of The Mountain* with a music video directed by Jimmy Murakami, which featured newspaper headlines reporting the death of Elvis. The single's cover art featured a drawing by Kate's young son Albert, who everyone called Bertie.

In the UK, *King Of The Mountain* made its chart debut at no.4, to give Kate her first Top 10 hit since *Don't Give Up* in 1986. Elsewhere, the single achieved no.3 in Finland, no.13 in Ireland and the Netherlands, no.24 in Italy, no.42 in Germany and no.47 in Switzerland.

In the UK and continental Europe, *King Of The Mountain* was released as a limited edition 7" picture disc single.

For the B-side of *King Of The Mountain*, Kate recorded a cover of Marvin Gaye's 1982 hit, *Sexual Healing*, which charted at no.1 in Canada and New Zealand, no.2 in Belgium, no.3 in the Netherlands and the United States, no.4 in Australia and the UK, and no.7 in Ireland.

Surprisingly, given its success, *King Of The Mountain* was the only single Kate released from her *AERIAL* album

CLASSIC**POP** PRESENTS

KATE BUSH

4OTH ANNIVERSARY EDITION

THIS WOMAN'S WORK

EXCLUSIVE INTERVIEWS • CLASSIC ALBUMS • RARE PHOTOS
COLLABORATIONS • HER GREATEST TRACKS AND MORE...

ANTHEM

THE ALMOST TOP 40 SINGLES

Only one of Kate's singles has made the Top 50 in one or more countries, but failed to enter the Top 40 in any.

The Dreaming

Kate wrote and produced *The Dreaming* herself, and she recorded the song for her album with the same title, released in 1982. Among the instruments heard on *The Dreaming* is the digeridoo, played by the then popular Australian artist and singer Rolf Harris, who was later found guilty of 12 counts of indecent assault, and on 4th July 2014 was sentenced to serve five years and nine months in prison in the UK.

 The Dreaming was issued as the follow-up to *Sat In Your Lap*, which had been released over a year previously. The single made its chart debut in the UK at no.49, and the following week it climbed one place to no.48, which proved to be its peak position. The single also spent a solitary week at no.91 in Australia, but it wasn't a hit anywhere else.

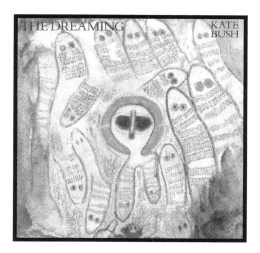

Note: To date, none of Kate's albums have entered the Top 50, but failed to achieved Top 40 status, anywhere.

Rolli **Stone**

Ausgabe 320 ›› Juni 2021
D: 7,90 € ›› A: 8,70 € ›› CH: 14,50 SFR

Das große
80er
Special

KATE BUSH

Ihr Triumph mit „Hounds Of Love"

& *die Lieblings-Alben der Redaktion*

LIZ
PHAIR

ASHE

VAN
MORRISON

JAN
DELAY

GARBAGE

WOLF
ALICE

JONI MITCHELL

Wie „Blue" die Welt veränderte

NOEL GALLAGHER

„Ich bin seit meiner Geburt im Lockdown"

96

KATE's TOP 20 SINGLES

In this Top 20, each of Kate's singles has been scored according to the following points system.

Points are given according to the peak position reached on the albums chart in each of the countries featured in this book:

No.1:	100 points for the first week at no.1, plus 10 points for each additional week at no.1.
No.2:	90 points for the first week at no.2, plus 5 points for each additional week at no.2.
No.3:	85 points.
No.4-6:	80 points.
No.7-10:	75 points.
No.11-15:	70 points.
No.16-20:	65 points.
No.21-30:	60 points.
No.31-40:	50 points.
No.41-50:	40 points.
No.51-60:	30 points.
No.61-70:	20 points.
No.71-80:	10 points.
No.81-100:	5 points.

Total weeks charted in each country are added, to give the final points score.

Reissues, re-entries and re-recordings of a single are counted together.

1   *Running Up That Hill* ~ 2,226 points

2   *Wuthering Heights* ~ 1,775 points

3   *Babooshka* ~ 909 points

4   *Don't Give Up* ~ 681 points

5   *The Sensual World* ~ 518 points

6. *Rocket Man* ~ 500 points
7. *Rubberband Girl* ~ 497 points
8. *King Of The Mountain* ~ 488 points
9. *The Man With The Child In His Eyes* ~ 393 points
10. *Cloudbusting* ~ 373 points

11. *Hammer Horror* ~ 337 points
12. *On Stage* EP ~ 303 points
13. *Sat In Your Lap* ~ 278 points
14. *Army Dreamers* ~ 219 points
15. *Experiment IV* ~ 184 points

16. *December Will Be Magic Again* ~ 177 points
17. *Hounds Of Love* ~ 175 points
18. *Wow* ~ 151 points
19. *This Woman's Work* ~ 134 points
20. *The Big Sky* ~ 127 points

Thanks to its revival in 2022, when it enjoyed far greater success than it had in 1985 on its original release, *Running Up That Hill (A Deal With God)* has overtaken *Wuthering Heights*, to become Kate's most successful chart single by some margin. *Babooshka. Don't Give Up* and *The Sensual World* round off the Top 5.

Kate's most recent single to make the Top 20 is *King of The Mountain*, which is at no.8.

THE ULTIMATE MUSIC GUIDE

KATE BUSH

DELUXE
REMASTERED
EDITION

CLASSIC
INTERVIEWS
EVERY
ALBUM
REVIEWED

Into The Sensual World

KATE BUSH: THE
WHOLE STORY

UNCUT ULTIMATE GUIDE SERIES
DECEMBER 2017 | UNCUT £15 UK

SINGLES TRIVIA

To date, Kate has achieved 27 Top 40 singles in one or more of the countries featured in this book.

There follows a country-by-country look at the most successful hits by Kate, starting with her homeland.

KATE IN THE UK

Kate has achieved 30 hit singles in the UK, which spent 229 weeks on the chart.

No.1 Singles

| 1978 | *Wuthering Heights* |
| 2022 | *Running Up That Hill (A Deal With God)* |

Most weeks at No.1

| 4 weeks | *Wuthering Heights* |
| 3 weeks | *Running Up That Hill (A Deal With God)* |

Note: had it not been for ACR (Accelerated Chart Ratio), which reduces streaming 'sales' by half for vintage tracks after three weeks of decline, *Running Up That Hill (A Deal With God)* would have topped the chart for six weeks.

Singles with the most weeks

50 weeks	*Running Up That Hill*
14 weeks	*Wuthering Heights*
11 weeks	*The Man With The Child In His Eyes*
11 weeks	*Don't Give Up*
10 weeks	*Wow*
10 weeks	*Babooshka*
9 weeks	*On Stage* EP
9 weeks	*Army Dreamers*
8 weeks	*Cloudbusting*
8 weeks	*Rocket Man*

The Brit Certified/BPI (British Phonographic Industry) Awards

The BPI began certifying Silver, Gold & Platinum singles in 1973. From 1973 to 1988: Silver = 250,000, Gold = 500,000 & Platinum = 1 million. From 1989 onwards: Silver = 200,000, Gold = 400,000 & Platinum = 600,000. Awards are based on shipments, not sales; however, in July 2013 the BPI automated awards, based on actual sales (including streaming 'sales' since February 1994.

2 x Platinum	*Running Up That Hill (A Deal With God)* (December 2021) = 1.2 million	
Gold & Platinum	*Wuthering Heights* (March 1978) = 500,000, (February 2022) = 600,000 Total = 1.1 million	
Gold	*This Woman's Work* (July 2022) = 400,000	
Silver	*Babooshka* (August 1980) = 250,000	
Silver	*Cloudbusting* (September 2021) = 200,000	
Silver	*Hounds Of Love* (September 2022) = 200,000	

KATE IN AUSTRALIA

Kate has achieved 11 hit singles in Australia, which spent 160 weeks on the chart.

No.1 Singles

1978	*Wuthering Heights*
2022	*Running Up That Hill (A Deal With God)*

Most weeks at No.1

9 weeks	*Running Up That Hill (A Deal With God)*
3 weeks	*Wuthering Heights*

Singles with the most weeks

38 weeks	*Running Up That Hill (A Deal With God)*
23 weeks	*Don't Give Up*
21 weeks	*Wuthering Heights*
21 weeks	*Babooshka*
19 weeks	*The Man With The Child In His Eyes*
14 weeks	*Hammer Horror*
14 weeks	*Rocket Man*

KATE IN AUSTRIA

Kate has achieved three hit singles in Austria, which spent 32 weeks on the chart.

Her most successful single is *Running Up That Hill (A Deal With God)*, which peaked at no.3 in 2022.

Singles with the most weeks

26 weeks   *Running Up That Hill (A Deal With God)*
4 weeks   *Wuthering Heights*
2 weeks   *King Of The Mountain*

KATE IN BELGIUM (Flanders)

Kate has achieved six hit singles in Belgium (Flanders), which spent 46 weeks on the chart.

Her most successful singles are *Wuthering Heights and Running Up That Hill (A Deal With God)*, which both peaked at no.6.

Singles with the most weeks

14 weeks   *Running Up That Hill (A Deal With God)*
11 weeks   *Wuthering Heights*
 7 weeks   *Don't Give Up*
 7 weeks   *The Sensual World*
 6 weeks   *Cloudbusting*

KATE IN CANADA

Kate has achieved five hit singles in Canada, which spent 60 weeks on the chart.

Her most successful single is *Running Up That Hill (A Deal With God)*, which spent two weeks at no.2 in 2022.

Singles with the most weeks

44 weeks   *Running Up That Hill A Deal With God)*
13 weeks   *Don't Give Up*
10 weeks   *Rubberband Girl*

8 weeks	*The Sensual World*
5 weeks	*Hounds Of Love*

KATE IN DENMARK

Kate has only achieved two hit singles in Denmark, which spent 19 weeks on the chart.

Her highest charting single is *Wuthering Heights*, which peaked at no.5 in 1978.

Singles with the most weeks

13 weeks	*Running Up That Hill (A Deal With God)*
6 weeks	*Wuthering Heights*

KATE IN FINLAND

Kate has achieved three hits singles in Finland, which spent 28 weeks on the chart.

Her most successful single is *Wuthering Heights*, which peaked at no.2.

Singles with the most weeks

13 weeks	*Running Up That Hill (Running Up That Hill)*
12 weeks	*Wuthering Heights*
3 weeks	*King Of The Mountain*

KATE IN FRANCE

Kate has achieved seven hit singles in France, which spent 116 weeks on the chart.

Her most successful single is *Running Up That Hill (A Deal With God)*, which peaked at no.3 in 2022.

Singles with the most weeks

39 weeks	*Running Up That Hill (A Deal With God)*
27 weeks	*Babooshka*
26 weeks	*Wuthering Heights*
16 weeks	*Suspended In Gaffa*
6 weeks	*Rocket Man*

KATE IN GERMANY

Kate has achieved 12 hit singles in Germany, which spent 171 weeks on the chart.

Her most successful single is *Running Up That Hill*, which peaked at no.3 in 1985.

Singles with the most weeks

50 weeks	*Running Up That Hill (A Deal With God)*
26 weeks	*Babooshka*
21 weeks	*Wuthering Heights*
14 weeks	*The Sensual World*
12 weeks	*Cloudbusting*
11 weeks	*Don't Give Up*
9 weeks	*Rocket Man*
8 weeks	*Rubberband Girl*

KATE IN IRELAND

Kate has achieved 20 hit singles in Ireland, which spent 112 weeks on the chart

No.1 Singles

1978	*Wuthering Heights*
2022	*Running Up That Hill (A Deal With God)*

Most weeks at No.1

7 weeks	*Running Up That Hill (A Deal With God)*
3 weeks	*Wuthering Heights*

Singles with the most weeks

38 weeks	*Running Up That Hill (A Deal With God)*
7 weeks	*Wuthering Heights*
7 weeks	*Army Dreamers*
6 weeks	*The Man With The Child In His Eyes*
6 weeks	*Wow*
5 weeks	*December Will Be Magic Again*
5 weeks	*Don't Give Up*

KATE IN ITALY

Kate has achieved seven hit singles in Italy, which spent 79 weeks on the chart.

No.1 Singles

1978   *Wuthering Heights*

Wuthering Heights topped the chart for one week.

Singles with the most weeks

26 weeks   *Wuthering Heights*
20 weeks   *Babooshka*
18 weeks   *Running Up That Hill (A Deal With God)*
 8 weeks   *The Sensual World*

KATE IN JAPAN

None of Kate's singles have charted in the Top 100 in Japan.

KATE IN THE NETHERLANDS

Kate has achieved 16 hit singles in the Netherlands, which spent 137 weeks on the chart.

Her highest charting singles are *Wuthering Heights* and *Running Up That Hill (A Deal With God)*, which both peaked at no.3.

Singles with the most weeks

31 weeks   *Running Up That Hill (A Deal With God)*
16 weeks   *Don't Give Up*
11 weeks   *The Man With The Child In His Eyes*
10 weeks   *The Sensual World*
 9 weeks   *Rocket Man*
 8 weeks   *Wuthering Heights*
 8 weeks   *On Stage* EP
 8 weeks   *Babooshka*
 8 weeks   *Army Dreamers*
 8 weeks   *Cloudbusting*

KATE IN NEW ZEALAND

Kate has achieved seven hit singles in New Zealand, which spent 87 weeks on the chart

No.1 Singles

1978	*Wuthering Heights*
2022	*Running Up That Hill (A Deal With God)*

Most weeks at No.1

5 weeks	*Wuthering Heights*
2 weeks	*Running Up That Hill (A Deal With God)*

Singles with the most weeks

25 weeks	*Running Up That Hill (A Deal With God)*
20 weeks	*Wuthering Heights*
14 weeks	*Don't Give Up*
13 weeks	*Babooshka*
9 weeks	*Hammer Horror*

KATE IN NORWAY

Kate has achieved three hit singles in Norway, which spent 31 weeks on the chart.

Her highest charting singles are *Babooshka* and *Running Up That Hill (A Deal With God)*, which both peaked at no.4.

Singles with the most weeks

13 weeks	*Running Up That Hill (A Deal With God)*
10 weeks	*Wuthering Heights*
8 weeks	*Babooshka*

KATE IN SOUTH AFRICA

Kate has achieved two hit singles in South Africa, which spent 19 weeks on the chart.

Her most successful single is *Wuthering Heights*, which peaked at no.3 in 1978.

Singles with the most weeks

11 weeks   *Wuthering Heights*
8 weeks   *Babooshka*

KATE IN SPAIN

Kate has achieved two hit singles in Spain, which spent 19 weeks on the chart.

Her highest charting single is *Wuthering Heights*, which peaked at no.10 in 1978.

Singles with the most weeks

10 weeks   *Running Up That Hill (A Deal With God)*
9 weeks   *Wuthering Heights*

KATE IN SWEDEN

Kate has achieved two hit singles in Sweden, which spent 33 weeks on the chart.

No.1 Singles

2022   *Running Up That Hill (A Deal With God)*

Running Up That Hill (A Deal With God) topped the chart for one week.

Singles with the most weeks

21 weeks   *Running Up That Hill (A Deal With God)*
12 weeks   *Wuthering Heights*

KATE IN SWITZERLAND

Kate has achieved four hit singles in Switzerland, which spent 64 weeks on the chart.

No.1 Singles

2022   *Running Up That Hill (A Deal With God)*

Running Up That Hill (A Deal With God) topped the chart for one week.

Singles with the most weeks

34 weeks	*Running Up That Hill (A Deal With God)*
13 weeks	*Wuthering Heights*
12 weeks	*Rocket Man*

KATE IN THE USA

Kate has achieved four hit singles in the United States, which spent 56 weeks on the Hot 100.

Her most successful single is *Running Up That Hill (A Deal With God)*, which peaked at no.3 in 2022.

Singles with the most weeks

40 weeks	*Running Up That Hill A Deal With God)*
6 weeks	*Don't Give Up*
6 weeks	*Rubberband Girl*
4 weeks	*The Man With The Child In His Eyes*

RIAA (Recording Industry Association of America) Awards

The RIAA began certifying Gold singles in 1958 and Platinum singles in 1976. From 1958 to 1988: Gold = 1 million, Platinum = 2 million. From 1988 onwards: Gold = 500,000, Platinum = 1 million. Awards are based on shipments, not sales (unless the award is for digital sales).

No singles by Kate have been certified.

THE ULTIMATE MUSIC GUIDE

KATE BUSH

NO.1 · RUNNING UP THAT HILL · RUNNING UP THAT HILL ·

CLASSIC
INTERVIEWS

EVERY
ALBUM
REVIEWED

KATE AND
*STRANGER
THINGS*:
HOW IT HAPPENED!

THE **VIDEOS**

THE **SINGLES**

THE **RARITIES**

BEFORE
THE DAWN

WOW!
KATE BUSH:
The whole story

FROM THE MAKERS OF **UNCUT**

All The Top 40 Albums

Record Mirror

**Kate
Bush**
Yes...
and she's only 19

Bowie dates
Rod in colour
Stranglers
E.L.O.

1 ~ THE KICK INSIDE

Moving/The Saxophone Song/Strange Phenomena/Kite/The Man With The Child In His Eyes/Wuthering Heights/James And The Cold Gun/Feel It/Oh To Be In Love/L'Amour Looks Something Like You/Them Heavy People/Room For Life/The Kick Inside

Produced by Andrew Powell; *The Saxophone Song & The Man With The Child In His Eyes* co-produced by David Gilmour.

UK: EMI EMC 3223 (1978).

11.03.78: 16-8-4-**3-3**-5-7-11-13-16-19-22-35-38-19-14-10-8-5-4-**3**-5-7-9-17-17-21-29-32-29-31-30-37-54

Pos	LW	Title, Artist			Peak Pos	WoC
1	1		**20 GOLDEN GREATS - BUDDY HOLLY AND THE CRICKETS** BUDDY HOLLY AND THE CRICKETS	EMI	1	4
2	2		**THE ALBUM** ABBA	EPIC	1	9
3	4 ↑		**THE KICK INSIDE** KATE BUSH	EMI	3	4

9.12.78: 74-x-73-73-x-62-67-64-72-51-62-42-37-40-66-57-36-49-36-36-26-21-23-40-33-

43-59-47-58
6.10.79: 75-65-51-55-58-57
23.08.80: 73
30.08.14: 87-24-42-69

Australia
24.04.78: peaked at no.**3**, charted for 41 weeks

Canada
3.06.78: 100-98-**95**-96

Finland
04.78: peaked at no.**2**, charted for 27 weeks

Germany
1.07.78: 28-33-30-36-**21**-31-33-37-38-40

Italy
2.09.78: peaked at no.**12**, charted for 13 weeks

Japan
20.05.78: peaked at no.**37**, charted for 14 weeks

Netherlands
25.03.78: 12-2-**1-1**-2-4-4-4-5-8-15-17-14-17-17-17-16-9-15-17-14-21-21-23-11-25-24-26-24-36

New Zealand
7.05.78: 5-3-3-**2**-4-4-4-4-5-7-8-13-16-29-29-x-29-35-35-x-23-x-37-37-12-7-7-14-11-25-26-35-30

Norway
8.04.78: 19-16-9-5-7-7-6-6-5-**4**-5-6-6-9-10-10-15-15-9-9-9-14-14-14-17

Sweden
21.04.78: 16-12-9-11-10-**8**-9-12-23-34

Kate was the sole composer of all 13 tracks she recorded for her debut album, *THE KICK INSIDE*.

'The album is something that has not just suddenly happened,' she said. 'It's been years of work because since I was a kid, I've always been writing songs and it was really just collecting together all the best songs that I had and putting them on the album, really years of preparation and inspiration that got it together.'

Two songs, *The Saxophone Song* and *The Man With The Child In His Eyes*, were three years old by the time the album was released, and were songs Kate originally worked on with Pink Floyd's David Gilmour, before she signed with EMI. The remaining tracks were recorded at London's AIR Studio in July and August 1977.

'When we were getting it together,' said Kate, 'one of the most important things that was on all our mind was, that because there were so many, we wanted to try and get as much variation as we could. To a certain extent, the actual songs allowed this because of the tempo changes, but there were certain songs that had to have a funky rhythm and there were others that had to be very subtle. I was very greatly helped by my producer and arranger, Andrew Powell, who really is quite incredible at tuning in to my songs. We made sure that there was one of the tracks, just me and the piano, to, again, give the variation. We've got a rock 'n' roll number in there, which again was important. And all the others there are just really the moods of the songs set with instruments, which for me is the most important thing, because you can so often get a beautiful song, but the arrangements can completely spoil it ~ they have to really work together.'

Kate wasn't afraid to include songs with unusual, potentially controversial subject matter, either. The album's title track, for example, was about the incestuous relationship between a brother and his sister.

'It was an area that I wanted to explore,' said Kate, 'because it's one that is really untouched and that is one of incest. There are so many songs about love, but they are always on such an obvious level. This song is about a brother and a sister who are in love, and the sister becomes pregnant by her brother. And because it is so taboo and unheard of, she kills herself in order to preserve her brother's name in the family. The actual song is in fact the suicide note. The sister is saying "I'm doing it for you" and "Don't worry, I'll come back to you someday".'

Kate was also involved with the sleeve design for *THE KICK INSIDE*.

'I think it went a bit over the top, actually,' she admitted. 'We had the kite, and as there is a song on the album by that name, and as the kite is traditionally Oriental, we painted the dragon on. But I think the lettering was just a bit too much … On the whole, I was surprised at the amount of control I actually had with the album production.'

Different sleeve designs were released in several countries, including Canada (top left), the United States, Japan (top right), Uruguay and Yugoslavia.

The rarest and most sought after edition of *THE KICK INSIDE* was released in Uruguay, with a monochrome photo.

THE KICK INSIDE was also released as a limited edition picture disc, in two slightly different editions.

There was only a relatively short, nine month gap between *THE KICK INSIDE* and Kate's second album, *LIONHEART*. This meant, in most countries, only two singles were released from *THE KICK INSIDE*:

- *Wuthering Heights*
- *The Man With The Child In His Eyes*

In the Far East, including Japan, *Moving* and *Them Heavy People* were promoted as singles, while *Strange Phenomena* was released in Brazil only.

THE KICK INSIDE spent three non-consecutive weeks at no.3 in the UK, and has spent well over a year on the chart. In selling more than a million copies, it is one of the country's best-selling albums by a British female singer-songwriter.

THE KICK INSIDE hit no.1 in the Netherlands, and charted at no.2 in Finland and New Zealand, no.3 in Australia, no.4 in Norway, no.8 in Sweden, no.12 in Italy, no.21 in Germany and no.37 in Japan. The album was a minor no.95 hit in Canada, but it failed to enter the Billboard 200 in the United States.

2 ~ LIONHEART

Symphony In Blue/In Search Of Peter Pan/Wow/Don't Push Your Foot On The Heartbrake/Oh England My Lionheart/Fullhouse/In The Warm Room/Kashka From Baghdad/Coffee Homeground/Hammer Horror

Produced by Andrew Powell, assisted by Kate Bush.

UK: EMI EMA 787 (1978).

25.11.78: 36-**6**-8-9-14-14-21-20-28-30-22-27-30-48-52-48-44-24-27-15-12-13-13-14-13-
    16-22-26-33-36-47-45-63-69-67-x-58
6.09.14: 40-60

Australia
27.11.78: peaked at no.**12**, charted for 18 weeks

Finland
12.78: peaked at no.**26**, charted for 6 weeks

Germany
25.12.78: 45-x-x-x-**25**-x-39-45-x-x-50

Japan
20.12.78: peaked at no.**30**, charted for 13 weeks

SHE'S HERE

THE KICK INSIDE EMC 3223

LIONHEART   EMA 787

ON TOUR
April
3rd Liverpool Empire
4th/5th Birmingham Hippodrome
6th Oxford New Theatre
7th Southampton Gaumont
9th Bristol Hippodrome
10th/11th Manchester Apollo
12th Sunderland Empire
13th Edinburgh Usher Hall
16th/17th/18th/19th/20th London Palladium

KATE BUSH.

Netherlands
25.11.78: 48-6-**5**-9-17-20-24-24-25-31-38-48

New Zealand
10.12.78: 6-**5-5-5-5-5**-13-21-31-38

Norway
2.12.78: 7-**5**-6-8-8-8-8-16-10-9-12-8-13-16-22

Sweden
1.12.78: 20-**16**-42-46-49

Kate's second album *LIONHEART* was released just nine months after her first, *THE KICK INSIDE*.

'I felt really squashed in by the lack of time,' admitted Kate, 'and that's what I don't like, especially if it's concerning something as important to me as my songs.'

Taking David Gilmour's advice, Kate flew to France to record her new album, at the Super Bear Studios in Berre-les-Alpes. However, things didn't go as she planned or wanted, as she and producer Andrew Powell clashed over which musicians would play on the album.

Kate wanted her own KT Bush band, which she had formed and played with between March and August 1977, before she signed with EMI, to play on her new album, but Andrew Powell had other ideas.

Kate actually recorded six songs with the KT Bush band, before Andrew Powell arrived in France ~ with the backing band he wanted to play on the album, comprising David Paton, Ian Bairnson and Stuart Elliott.

'Andrew Powell reined us in quite severely,' said Charlie Morgan, a member of the KT Bush band. 'There was a little bit of subterfuge going on, too. He (Andrew Powell) had signed a deal to produce the second album, and naturally wanted his boys to do it. Kate was adamant that she wanted us to do the album, so we were caught in the middle of a tug-of-war.'

Kate, this time, didn't get her own way as EMI sided with Andrew Powell. This meant, to her dismay, the songs she had already recorded with the KT Bush band had to be re-cut.

Due to time constraints, Kate only wrote three new songs for *LIONHEART*: *Coffee Homeground*, *Fullhouse* and *Symphony In Blue*.

'There were quite a few old songs that I managed to get the time to re-write,' said Kate. 'It's a much lighter level of work when you re-write a song because the basic inspiration is there, you just perfect upon it and that's great … In fact, we ended up with more than we needed again, which is fantastic.'

Kate recorded a dozen songs in France, and what were considered the best ten were chosen for her new album, which she decided to title *LIONHEART* after one of the tracks on the album, *Oh England My Lionheart*. The album's sleeve was designed around the same theme.

'We wanted to get across a vibe within me of a lion,' said Kate. 'And for the front cover it basically comes from an idea that my brother had, which was an attic setting with me in a lion suit, so it's slightly comical, but just a really nice vibe on the front that would take away the heavy, crusader, English vibe, because Lionheart is always associated with Richard the Lionheart.'

LIONHEART produced two Top 40 singles:

* *Hammer Horror*
* *Wow*

A third single, *Symphony In Blue*, was issued in Canada and Japan only ~ it Canada, with *Hammer Horror* as the B-side, it was issued on blue vinyl. *Symphony In Blue* wasn't a hit.

Although not as successful as *THE KICK INSIDE*, *LIONHEART* did achieve no.5 in the Netherlands, New Zealand and Norway, no.6 in the UK, no.12 in Australia, no.16 in Sweden, no.25 in Germany, no.26 in Finland and no.30 in Japan.

With hindsight, however, Kate wasn't entirely happy with her second album.

'Looking back,' she reflected, 'I don't really think that *LIONHEART* actually expressed the true phase I was in at the time, whereas all the others have. While the first LP consisted of material I'd written up to that point, I found that the time pressures prevented me from writing more fresh material for the second one.'

3 ~ NEVER FOR EVER

Babooshka/Delius/Blow Away/All We Ever Look For/Egypt/The Wedding List/Violin/The Infant Kiss/Night Scented Stock/Army Dreamers/Breathing

Produced by Kate Bush & Jon Kelly.

UK: EMI EMA 794 (1980).

20.09.80: **1**-2-3-6-5-7-9-10-19-30-36-32-40-35-40-40-44-34-44-50-62-63-72

Pos	LW	Title, Artist		Peak Pos	WoC
1	New	**NEVER FOR EVER** KATE BUSH	EMI	1	1
2	2	**SIGNING OFF** UB40	GRADUATE	2	3
3	1 ↓	**TELEKON** GARY NUMAN	BEGGARS BANQUET	1	2

6.09.14: 38-78

Australia
6.10.80: peaked at no.**7**, charted for 20 weeks

Canada
8.11.80: 91-91-69-? 47-47-**44**

Germany
29.09.80: 52-39-**5**-7-11-16-14-11-12-13-11-18-21-20-21-22-16-17-20-21-32-28-36-32-36-
  47-52-49-52-56-57

Japan
21.09.80: peaked at no.**40**, charted for 8 weeks

Netherlands
20.09.80: 17-**4**-5-9-8-**4**-6-10-9-8-10-9-12-17-16-21-25-46

New Zealand
26.10.80: 38-45-36-x-x-50-x-35-38-38-38-38-**31**-40-49

Norway
20.09.80: 12-5-6-**2-2-2**-5-8-10-10-18-24-26-30-28-28-28-28-26-27

Sweden
3.10.80: **16**-18-29

After working with producer Andrew Powell on her first two albums, Kate felt confident enough to take on the role of lead producer herself on her third album, with Jon Kelly co-producing.

'It means I have more control over my album,' she said, 'which is going to make it more rounded, more complete, more me, I hope.'

Kate's Tour Of Life concluded at London's Hammersmith Odeon on 14th May 1979. After taking a short break, she started work on her new album in September, recording at two London studios, Abbey Road and AIR. Kate composed all eleven songs she recorded for the album, which was completed in May 1980.

'Its name is *NEVER FOR EVER*,' Kate revealed, 'and I've called it this because I've tried to make it reflective of all that happens to you and me. Life, love, hate, we are all transient. All things pass, neither good nor evil lasts. So we must tell our hearts that it is "never for ever" and be happy that it's like that!'

The album's distinctive cover was designed by Nick Price.

'On the cover of *NEVER FOR EVER*,' explained Kate, 'Nick takes us on an intricate journey of our emotions: inside gets outside, as we flood people and things with our desires and problems. These black and white thoughts, these bats and doves, freeze-framed in flight, swoop into the album and out of your hi-fis. Then it's for you to bring them to life.'

NEVER FOR EVER produced three hit singles:

- *Breathing*
- *Babooshka*
- *Army Dreamers*

The track *Blow Away* was dedicated to Kate's lighting director, Bill Duffield, who was tragically killed at the Poole Arts Centre, during Kate's Tour Of Life. The song links Bill's name to the names of several iconic music stars who are also no longer with us, including Buddy Holly, Keith Moon, Marc Bolan, Minnie Riperton, Sandy Denny and Sid Vicious.

In the UK, *NEVER FOR EVER* became the first album by a female artist to enter the UK's album chart at no.1. It was also the first studio album, as opposed to a compilation album, by a female artist to top the chart and was, of course, Kate's first no.1 album.

NEVER FOR EVER spent three consecutive weeks at no.2 in Norway, and achieved no.4 in the Netherlands, no.5 in Germany, no.7 in Australia, no.16 in Sweden, no.31 in New Zealand, no.40 in Japan and no.44 in Canada.

4 ~ THE DREAMING

Sat In Your Lap/There Goes A Tenner/Pull Out The Pin/Suspended In Gaffa/Leave It Open/The Dreaming/Night Of The Swallow/All The Love/Houdini/Get Out Of My House

Produced by Kate Bush.

UK: EMI EMC 3419 (1982).

25.09.82: **3**-8-15-18-32-42-59-57-74-85

Pos	LW	Title, Artist		Peak Pos	WoC
1	1	**THE KIDS FROM FAME** KIDS FROM FAME	BBC	1	10
2	7 ↑	**CHARTBEAT/CHARTHEAT** VARIOUS ARTISTS (K-TEL)	K-TEL	2	3
3	New	**THE DREAMING** KATE BUSH	EMI	3	1

6.09.14: 37-53

Australia
11.10.82: peaked at no.**22**, charted for 10 weeks

127

Canada
16.10.82: 88-66-52-41-37-33-**29-29**-31-42-47-47-47-62-72-82-84

Germany
11.10.82: 40-**23**-39-27-38-36-34-39-38-43-40-49-54-52-65-60-60-62-63

Japan
1.10.82: peaked at no.**36**, charted for 7 weeks

Netherlands
25.09.82: 37-6-**5**-8-23-30-x-45
25.12.82: 49-x-x-47-50

Norway
18.09.82: 29-15-19-**12**-18-26-27

Sweden
28.09.82: 49-x-x-x-**45**

Kate started writing new songs for what would be her fourth album in September 1980, but it was May 1982 before *THE DREAMING* was finally completed.

'I started writing some new songs,' she said. 'They were very different from anything I'd ever written before ~ they were much more rhythmic, and in a way, a completely new side to my music. I was using different instruments, and everything was changing, and I felt that really the best thing to do would be to make this album a real departure ~ make it completely different.'

In order to achieve her aim, after working closely with Jon Kelly on her previous album, Kate decided to take complete control and produce an album herself for the first time.

'The only way to achieve this' she explained, 'was to sever all the links I had had with the older stuff. The main link was engineer Jon Kelly. Every time I was in the studio Jon was there helping me, so I felt that in order to make the stuff different enough I would have to stop working with Jon. He really wanted to keep working with me, but we discussed it and realised that it was for the best.'

Kate described *THE DREAMING* as a 'very dark' album that was about pain and negativity, and the way people treat each other badly. Of course, the fact she was in total control meant, for the first time, she could do what she really wanted to do without having to answer to anyone else.

'The songs themselves were very demanding, especially emotionally,' said Kate, 'and they seemed to be requiring more special sounds, new treatment, that sort of thing, so it was harder to find sounds that were right and it took longer to get ideas manifested. And also, I was having to work between three or four studios in order to be able to get the time to make sure that the impetuous was carried on and the album was finished, because I was making an album at the same time a lot of other people were and obviously everybody wanted to use the same top studios in London, so I was having to move around a lot, which was hard.'

The four London studios Kate recorded *THE DREAMING* at were Abbey Road Studios, Advision Studios, Odyssey Studios and Townhouse Studios.

Five singles were released from *THE DREAMING* in various different countries:

- *Sat In Your Lap*
- *The Dreaming*
- *Suspended In Gaffa*
- *There Goes A Tenner*
- *Night Of The Swallow*

Of the five, only *Sat In Your Lap* and *Suspended In Gaffa* achieved Top 40 status anywhere, although *The Dreaming* came close. *There Goes A Tenner* was only issued in Ireland and the UK, and was a minor no.93 hit in the UK, while *Night Of The Swallow* was released exclusively in Ireland and wasn't a hit.

THE DREAMING fared much better than the singles released from it, and charted at no.3 in the UK, no.5 in the Netherlands, no.12 in Norway, no.22 in Australia, no.23 in Germany, no.29 in Canada, no.36 in Japan and no.45 in Sweden.

5 ~ HOUNDS OF LOVE

Side 1 ~ Hounds Of Love: *Running Up That Hill (A Deal With God)/Hounds Of Love/The Big Sky/Mother Stands For Comfort/Cloudbusting*

Side 2 ~ The Ninth Wave: *And Dream Of Sheep/Under Ice/Waking The Witch/Watching You Without Me/Jig Of Life/Hello Earth/The Morning Fog*

Produced by Kate Bush.

UK: EMI KAB1 (1985).

28.09.85: **1-1**-2-**1**-5-4-5-9-20-22-28-28-29-32-28-24-27-30-32-32-36-19-14-9-6-6-13-19-24-23-43-30-29-28-32-36-36-39-46-51-61-67-70-79-80-60-65-63-65-83-82

Pos	LW	Title, Artist		Peak Pos	WoC
1	New	**HOUNDS OF LOVE** KATE BUSH	EMI	1	1
2	1 ↓	**LIKE A VIRGIN** MADONNA	SIRE	1	45
3	2 ↓	**NOW THAT'S WHAT I CALL MUSIC 5** VARIOUS ARTISTS	EMI/VIRGIN	1	7

13.10.01: 78-46

8.10.05: 62-69
30.08.14: 29-9-20-24-45-68-56-61
29.11.14: 99
16.06.22: 84-95-80

Australia
28.10.85: peaked at no.**6**, charted for 19 weeks

Austria
1.11.85: 26-15-**14-14**-17-29-28 (bi-weekly)

Belgium
11.06.22: 97

Canada
5.10.85: 94-79-45-36-28-16-13-8-**7**-8-8-8-14-14-14-14-15-19-22-25-29-39-47-48-48-54-
    59-65-82
11.06.22: 19-8-13-15-32-18-22-30-39-50-54-67-80-97-96-35

Denmark
15.06.22: **9**-23-28-34-24-24-26-31-36

Finland
09.85: peaked at no.**5**, charted for 14 weeks

Germany
30.09.85: 8-5-**2-2-2**-5-4-4-7-8-9-8-8-10-11-8-14-16-20-24-35-27-40-49-44-43-47-44-50-
    57-59-65

Zeitraum: **14.10.1985 - 20.10.1985**   ‹ ZURÜCK   VOR ›

1	1	**Peter Maffay** Sonne in der Nacht Teldec	IN CHARTS: **5 W** PEAK: **1**	🎧
2	5 ↑	**Kate Bush** Hounds Of Love EMI	IN CHARTS: **3 W** PEAK: **2**	🎧
3	2 ↓	**Madonna** Like A Virgin Sire (WEA)	IN CHARTS: **43 W** PEAK: **1**	🎧

Japan
28.09.85: peaked at no.**36**, charted for 11 weeks

Netherlands
28.09.85: 39-**1-1**-2-4-8-9-11-5-5-5-7-7-8-11-11-10-14-20-19-26-42-36-43-34-51-49-57-68

4.06.22: 18-6-4-8-7-8-9-7-6-8-12-23-40-40-52-70-95

New Zealand
27.10.85: 21-20-**17**-21-23-30-46-40-40-40-40-40-32-34-33-49-44-45-x-x-38-35

Norway
5.10.85: 16-**12-12**-20-20-20

Sweden
4.10.85: 17-10-**9**-12-31

Switzerland
13.10.85: 8-**3-3-3**-6-8-11-14-14-20-29

4.09.22: 60

USA
26.10.85: 74-51-38-33-33-32-31-30-41-41-41-48-48-57-57-59-62-67-72
11.06.22: 28-**12**-19-30-42-21-27-46-64-85-98-x-x-x-x-52

Kate started working on her fifth album, which became *HOUNDS OF LOVE*, in January 1984, and completed the album in June 1985.

'On this album,' she said, 'I wanted to get away from the energy of the last one ~ at the time I was very unhappy, I felt that mankind was really screwing things up. Having expressed all that, I wanted this album to be different ~ a positive album, just as personal but more about the good things. A lot depends on how you feel at any given time, it all comes out in the music.'

Although she worked at London's Abbey Road Studios and Dublin's Windmill Lane Studios, Kate recorded most of the album at her own Wickham Farm Home Studios, which was a 24-track studio she had built in a barn at her home during the summer of 1983. Having her own studio, she felt, was 'another step closer to getting the work as direct as possible. You cut all the crap, don't have all these people around and don't have expensive studio time mounting up.'

HOUNDS OF LOVE was an album of two parts.

'It's almost like two separate albums for me,' said Kate, 'in that the first side is five separate songs; if they're linked it's only be the theme of love ~ they're all forms of love songs, they're about relationships. They're all very different subject matters from each other. And the second side of the album is a conceptual piece which is seven songs all linked together, and it's very much something that was designed and written to work as one piece of music.'

Kate admitted there were times when she though the album would never be finished.

'It was just such a lot of work,' she said, 'all of it was so much work, you know, the lyrics, trying to piece the thing together, but I did love it. I did enjoy it and everyone that worked on the album was wonderful, and it was really, in some ways, I think, the happiest I've been when I'd been writing and making an album.'

For the album's cover, Kate wanted a photograph of herself with two hounds ~ which proved far more challenging than she anticipated.

'The two dogs are friends of ours' she said, 'and John, my brother, who took the photograph, had a lot of trouble keeping them under control. I think he had a very strong word with them and got them to behave, and it really was just a matter of patience, because we'd get the whole scene set up, and then the dogs would come in and they'd be walking all over me and everything, and it would be totally ruined in five minutes, so we'd have to start again.'

Four singles, all of them Top 40 hits, were released from *HOUNDS OF LOVE*:

- *Running Up That Hill*
- *Cloudbusting*

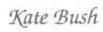

Kate Bush

The Hair of the Hound

- *Hounds Of Love*
- *The Big Sky*

The music videos for the four singles were issued in 1986 on a home video compilation titled *The Hair Of The Hound*.

HOUNDS OF LOVE gave Kate her second no.1 album in the UK, where it made its chart debut at no.1 and topped the chart for three non-consecutive weeks.

The album also went to no.1 in the Netherlands, and achieved no.2 in Germany, no.3 in Switzerland, no.5 in Finland, no.6 in Australia, no.7 in Canada, no.9 in Sweden, no.12 in Norway, no.14 in Austria, no.17 in New Zealand, no.30 in the United States and no.36 in Japan.

HOUNDS OF LOVE was nominated for three Brit Awards:

- Best British Album
- Best British Female
- Best British Single ~ *Running Up That Hill*

First Century Edition

HOUNDS OF LOVE was remastered and reissued in 1997, as part of EMI's First Century reissue series, with six bonus tracks (two remixes and four B-sides):

The Big Sky (Meteorogical Mix)/Running Up That Hill (12" Mix)/Be Kind To My Mistakes/Under The Ivy/Burning Bridge/My Lagan Love

HOUNDS OF LOVE, as well as being hugely successful, is Kate's most critically acclaimed album. In 2020, *Q* magazine ranked *HOUNDS OF LOVE* at no.20 in its 100 Greatest British Albums Ever listing, while *Rolling Stone* magazine had the album at no.68 in its Greatest Albums of All-Time listing.

In 2011, a Collector's Edition 10" vinyl EP, pressed on marbled pink vinyl, was released exclusively in the United States. Although titled *Hounds Of Love*, the four songs on the EP were *The Big Sky*, *Cloudbusting*, *Watching You Without Me* and *Jig Of Life*.

In 2021, as part of HMV's century vinyl 'Exclusives Day', 1500 copies of *HOUNDS OF LOVE* were pressed on recycled vinyl.

The success of *Running Up That Hill (A Deal With God)* in 2022, thanks to its inclusion in the *Stanger Things* TV show, saw *HOUNDS OF LOVE* charting in several countries ~ it peaked at no.4 in the Netherlands, no.8 in Canada, no.9 in Denmark and no.12 in the United States.

6 ~ THE WHOLE STORY

*Wuthering Heights (New Vocal)/Cloudbusting/The Man With The Child In His Eyes/
Breathing/Wow/Hounds Of Love/Running Up That Hill/Army Dreamers/Sat In Your
Lap/Experiment IV/The Dreaming/Babooshka*

UK: EMI KBTV 1 (1986).

22.11.86: 3-2-3-3-3-2-4-2-**1-1**-2-2-5-8-12-14-20-21-24-25-25-31-30-40-39-46-46-56-59-
66-67-70-72-76-81-93-85-85-67-72-82-94-76-95

Pos	LW	Title, Artist		Peak Pos	WoC
1	2 ↑	**THE WHOLE STORY** KATE BUSH	EMI	1	9
2	4 ↑	**GRACELAND** PAUL SIMON	WARNER BROTHERS	1	19
3	3	**TRUE BLUE** MADONNA	SIRE	1	28

29.05.93: 77-81
30.04.94: 71-x-x-x-48-59-56-90
17.09.94: 90-70-74-75-81-83-83-99
7.01.95: 70-72-84-81
22.03.97: 99

13.10.01: 45-62-78
3.04.04: 98
5.11.05: 94-93-88-88
29.04.06: 80-87-91-94
28.10.06: 74-96
9.06.07: 94
18.08.12: 92-21-29-47-42-47-64-66-84
5.04.14: 66-71-66-75-51-52-67-85-56-64-72-73-71-x-x-x-x-97-x-x-91-15-6-9-15-19-23-
    21-27-46-54-55-44-78-46-80-75-81-92-84-75-70-84-94-93-63-76-100-x-x-x-x-98-x-x-
    x-x-46
9.06.22: 76-19-24-17-27-28-38-58-65-28-41-74-93

Australia
8.12.86: peaked at no.**28**, charted for 28 weeks

Canada
6.12.86: 81-71-58-47-47-47-37-35-32-28-28-**27-27-27**-41-45-47-60-60-63-72-81-98

Finland
12.86: peaked at no.**33**, charted for 5 weeks

Germany
8.12.86: 23-25-17-20-18-**11**-17-24-30-32-36-35-51-48-48-50-49-60-62

Japan
20.12.86: peaked at no.**38**, charted for 10 weeks

Netherlands
29.11.86: 37-34-32-29-23-**22-22**-24-23-26-32-34-28-34-53-44-34-39-57
15.09.01: 90-55-61-69-75-80-74-79-99
26.04.14: 59
2.08.14: 59-86-69-73-74-45-52-82

New Zealand
14.12.96: 30-27-27-27-27-45-47-43-43-x-x-**4-4**-6-9-10-17-16-19-35-40-45-50-x-49

Norway
13.09.03: 36-**10**-17-28

Sweden
17.12.86: **48-48**

USA
24.01.87: 84-78-**76**-82-87-85-92-94-94-100

THE WHOLE STORY was Kate's first compilation album and, initially at least, she was against its release.

'I was concerned that it would be like a K-Tel record,' she said, 'a cheapo-compo with little thought behind it. It was the record company's decision, and I didn't mind as long as it was well put together. We put a lot of work into the packaging, trying to make it look tasteful, and carefully thought out the running order. And the response has been phenomenal ~ I'm amazed!'

One new song, *Experiment IV*, featured on *THE WHOLE STORY*, which opened with a newly recorded version of Kate's debut hit, *Wuthering Heights*.

'I wanted to put a contemporary mark on it,' said Kate. 'I felt it sounded like a very little girl singing that to me, and the production was very much a Seventies production. And although there were some other tracks in there that you could say the same thing of, they weren't as blatant as that one was. If I had had the time I probably would have done the same to some of the other tracks, but there was just no time ~ there was too much to do with recording and writing *Experiment IV*, plus doing the video. It was a very intense period to get that out on the deadline.'

THE WHOLE STORY was also released as a home video.

'I really like the idea of the album being available on video,' said Kate. 'I've always wanted to make a form of video album, but I never thought it would be a compilation!'

On the home video, rather than include the *Wow* promo, Kate decided to piece together footage from live shows instead, for two reasons.

'Firstly, I really don't like the promo we did for *Wow* ~ I think it's silly,' she explained. 'And also, looking through the videos I noticed a great absence of performance promos, and the tour was an important part of the story. Also, it makes it a more interesting item for people who have some of the other videos. That way, it's not just *Experiment IV* that is a new visual.'

The home video picked up a Grammy nomination, for Best Concept Music Video, but Kate lost out to Genesis, who took the award for their *Land Of Confusion* home video.

THE WHOLE STORY was hugely successful in the UK, where the compilation gave Kate her third no.1 album. The compilation topped the chart for two weeks, and has re-entered the chart numerous times over the years, accumulating an impressive 132 weeks on the Top 100 to date.

Around the world, *THE WHOLE STORY* achieved no.4 in New Zealand, no.10 in Norway, no.11 in Germany, no.22 in the Netherlands, no.27 in Canada, no.28 in Australia, no.33 in Finland, no.38 in Japan and no.48 in Sweden. The compilation was also a minor no.76 hit in the United States.

7 ~ THE SENSUAL WORLD

The Sensual World/Love And Anger/The Fog/Reaching Out/Heads We're Dancing/Deeper Understanding/Between A Man And A Woman/Never Be Mine/Rocket's Tail (For Rocket)/ This Woman's Work

CD Bonus Track: *Walk Straight Down The Middle*

Produced by Kate Bush.

UK: EMI EMD 1010 (1989).

28.10.89: **2**-6-15-23-24-31-32-26-21-16-27-36-38-44-51-55-66-66-72-70

Pos	LW	Title, Artist		Peak Pos	WoC
1	New	**WILD!** ERASURE	MUTE	1	1
2	New	**THE SENSUAL WORLD** KATE BUSH	EMI	2	1
3	1 ↓	**ENJOY YOURSELF** KYLIE MINOGUE	PWL	1	2

30.08.14: 93-26-39-75

Australia
12.11.89: 46-**30**-48-43

Canada
4.11.89: 59-19-15-18-23-17-17-**14-14-14**-30-24-23-23-38-38-37-51-53-65-90-98

Finland
10.89: peaked at no.**4**, charted for 12 weeks

Germany
30.10.89: 20-15-**10**-11-15-18-22-30-34-36-38-34-47-51-60-64-69-70-72-79-83

Italy
21.10.89: peaked at no.**14**, charted for 6 weeks

Japan
25.10.89: peaked at no.**18**, charted for 4 weeks

Netherlands
28.10.89: 69-24-18-17-**16**-20-29-38-48-69-79-83-89-95

New Zealand
10.12.89: **27**-44

Norway
28.10.89: 20-9-**7**-8-13-20

Sweden
1.11.89: **17-17**-28-50-x-x-x-49

Switzerland
12.11.89: 25-17-**11**-20-26

USA
4.11.89: 84-49-46-**43-43**-46-46-50-50-45-44-48-46-49-59-60-61-66-76-87

Kate wrote and recorded the 10 songs and the CD only bonus track featured on her sixth studio album, *THE SENSUAL WORLD*, between September 1987 and July 1989. She recorded the album at her own Wickham Farm Home Studios and Dublin's Windmill Lane Studios, and she produced the album herself.

'I think this album for me, unlike the last album, *HOUNDS OF LOVE*,' said Kate, 'where I saw that as two sides ~ one side being conceptual ~ this album is very much like short stories for me. Ten short stories that are just saying something different in each one and it was a bit like trying to paint the pictures accordingly. Each song has a different personality and so they each a need little bit of something here, a little bit of that there ~ just like people, you know, some people you can't walk up to because you know they're a bit edgy first thing in the morning, so you have to come up sideways to them, and it's kind of like how the songs are too. They have their own little personalities, and if it doesn't want you to do it, it won't let you.'

Both *THE DREAMING* and *HOUNDS OF LOVE*, Kate felt, were more male than female in terms of power and attitude. On her new album, she wanted to explore her feminine side more.

'I just felt that I was exploring my feminine energy more ~ *musically,*' she said. 'In the past I had wanted to emanate the kind of power that I've heard in male music, and I just felt maybe somewhere there is this female energy that's powerful. It's a subtle difference ~ male or female energy in art ~ but I think there *is* a difference. Little things, like using the Trio (Bulgarka), and possibly some of the attitudes to my lyric writing on this album. I would say it was more accepting of being a female somehow.'

As a result, in many ways Kate felt *THE SENSUAL WORLD* was her most personal album to date.

'I think a lot of that's directly to do with the way we worked on it.' she said. 'I think that having just the two of us in the studio (Kate and Del Palmer), being very isolated, has made it much easier for me to get things across, because I'm dealing with someone who knows what I'm trying to say, rather than three or four people who keep changing. The problem with commercial studios is that there are so many distractions and strangers, which makes me nervous. To be at home and be so relaxed, working with someone I know and love so much, gives it a very intimate and special feeling. It's not always easy, but I wouldn't have it any other way.'

Three singles, all of which achieved Top 40 status in at least one country, were released from *THE SENSUAL WORLD*:

- *The Sensual World*
- *This Woman's Work*
- *Love And Anger*

The music videos for the three hits, plus a 22 minute interview with Kate, were issued on a home video titled, *The Sensual World: The Videos.*

THE SENSUAL WORLD made its chart debut in the UK at no.2 ~ kept off the top spot by the new album by Erasure, *WILD!* The album also achieved no.4 in Finland, no.7 in Norway, no.10 in Germany, no.11 in Switzerland, no.14 in Canada and Italy, no.16 in the Netherlands, no.17 in Sweden, no.18 in Japan, no.27 in New Zealand, no.30 in Australia and no.43 in the United States.

In 1990, a five track EP titled *Aspects Of The Sensual World* was released exclusively in the United States. The five tracks on the CD were:

The Sensual World (LP Version), Be Kind To My Mistakes (From The Film 'Castaways'), I'm Still Waiting, Ken (From The Comic Strip Film 'G.L.C.') and The

Sensual World (Instrumental Mix).

THE SENSUAL WORLD picked up a Grammy nomination, for Best Alternative Music Album, but Kate lost out to Sinéad O'Connor's album, *I DO NOT WANT WHAT I HAVEN'T GOT*.

THE SENSUAL WORLD was reissued on blue vinyl in 2018, as part of UNICEF's vinyl project. Kate was one of more than a dozen artists who participated, and only 50 numbered copies of each album were pressed. All the albums were raffled off in a prize draw, with proceeds going to UNICEF's Children's Emergency Fund in the UK.

8 ~ THE RED SHOES

Rubberband Girl/And So Is Love/Eat The Music/Moments Of Pleasure/The Song Of Solomon/Lily/The Red Shoes/Top Of The City/Constellation Of The Heart/Big Stripey Lie/Why Should I Love You?/You're The One

Produced by Kate Bush.

UK: EMI CDEMD 1047 (1993).

13.11.93: **2**-8-14-16-17-19-21-19-23-20-22-22-33-42-63-76-96

Pos	LW	Title, Artist		Peak Pos	WoC
1	1	**BAT OUT OF HELL II - BACK INTO HELL** MEAT LOAF	VIRGIN	1	9
2	New	**RED SHOES** KATE BUSH	EMI	2	1
3	New	**FULL MOON, DIRTY HEARTS** INXS	MERCURY	3	1

6.09.14: 49-45

Australia
28.11.93: **17**-32-45

February 1978   November 1978   September 1980   September 1982   September 1985   November 1986   September 1989

1993

KATE BUSH

THE RED SHOES

features RUBBERBAND GIRL plus 11 new tracks

Austria
28.11.93: **34**-36-36-40

Canada
20.11.93: 19-**13**-**13**-14-25-38-38-44-82-77-71-67-63-79-73-83-98

Finland
11.93: peaked at no.**3**, charted for 13 weeks

Germany
15.11.93: 48-**18**-**18**-24-29-42-55-64-62-58

Japan
1.11.93: peaked at no.**24**, charted for 3 weeks

Netherlands
13.11.93: 86-36-**23**-32-41-50-58-55-67-67-88-98-98

New Zealand
20.11.93: **30**

Sweden
10.11.93: **16**-20-23-38

Switzerland
14.11.93: 35-36-**26**-34-x-x-49

USA
20.11.93: **28**-55-80

THE RED SHOES was Kate's seventh album. The album's title was inspired by the 1948 film with the same title.

Kate wrote and recorded the 12 songs on the album herself between June 1990 and June 1993 ~ she recorded the album at London's Abbey Road Studios.

To accompany the album, Kate also released a short film, *The Line, The Cross & The Curve*, which she wrote and directed herself. As well as Kate, the promo featured actress Miranda Richardson. The songs from the album featured in the short film were:

Rubberband Girl/And So Is Love/The Red Shoes/Lily/The Red Shoes (Instrumental)/ Moments Of Pleasure/Eat The Music/The Red Shoes

Footage from the short film served as promo music videos for the five songs that were issued as singles from the album, although Kate did also film an alternative *Rubberband Girl* promo for the North American market.

The Line, The Cross & The Curve was nominated for a Grammy, for Best Music Video, Long Form, but Kate lost out to Peter Gabriel and his *Secret World Live*.

Why Should I Love You? was a song Kate had sent to Prince, after she had attended one of his concerts at London's Earls Court in June 1992, and received a note from him saying how much he admired her work. Since Prince's busy schedule allowed him no time to visit Kate in England, she sent him some tapes of *Why Should I Love You?*, and asked him if would add some vocals to the song. Prince, however, did so much more.

'He'd looped a four-bar section from the chorus of the song that Kate had written,' said Del Palmer, 'and just smothered 48 tracks with everything you could possibly imagine ~ guitars, keyboards, drums, vocals. I just sat there and thought, "Well, this is great, but what are we going to do with it?".'

Kate and Del Palmer puzzled over the song, and what to do with it, for months. Eventually, since Prince hadn't added some vocals Kate wanted, she turned to an unlikely source, to ask him if he would add the vocals she wanted: comedian Lenny Henry!

'It was like he'd worked in the studio his whole life,' said Del Palmer. 'Kate sang him the part she wanted him to do and then he sang it. Then she asked him to do a harmony, which he worked out with her.'

Five singles were released from *THE RED SHOES* in various countries:

- *Rubberband Girl*
- *Eat The Music*
- *Moments Of Pleasure*
- *The Red Shoes*
- *And So Is Love*

Four of the single achieved Top 40 status in one or more countries, the one exception being *Eat The Music*, which failed to enter any mainstream chart but did rise to no.10 on Billboard's Alternative Airplay chart in the United States.

Eat The Music was originally planned as the album's lead single in the UK, and copies were pressed, with a picture sleeve, before the decision was taken to release *Rubberband Girl* instead ~ allegedly, only 17 copies of the cancelled single still exist.

Kate, originally, planned to tour to promote the release of *THE RED SHOES*, but ultimately the tour was shelved. Despite this, *THE RED SHOES*, made its chart debut at no.2 in the UK, only kept off the top spot by Meat Loaf's *BAT OUT OF HELL II – BACK INTO HELL*.

Around the world, *THE RED SHOES* charted at no.3 in Finland, no.13 in Canada, no.16 in Sweden, no.17 in Australia, no.18 in Germany, no.23 in the Netherlands, no.24 in Japan, no.26 in Switzerland, no.28 in the United States, no.30 in New Zealand and no.34 in Austria.

Following *THE RED SHOES*, Kate planned to take a year or so off, before she started working on a new album ~ however, it would be another 12 years before she released her next studio album.

9 ~ AERIAL

CD1 ~ A Sea Of Honey: *King Of The Mountain/π/Bertie/Mrs Bartolozzi/How To Be Invisible/Joanni/A Coral Room*

CD2 ~ A Sky Of Honey: *Prelude/Prologue/An Architect's Dream/This Painter's Link/Sunset/Aerial Tal/Somewhere In Between/Nocturn/Aerial*

Produced by Kate Bush.

UK: EMI KBACD 01 (2005).

19.11.05: **3**-8-25-34-36-37-38-51-54-55-59-82-67-72-60-71

Pos	LW	Title, Artist		Peak Pos	WoC
1	New	**ANCORA** IL DIVO	SYCO MUSIC	1	1
2	1↓	**FACE TO FACE** WESTLIFE	S	1	2
3	New	**AERIAL** KATE BUSH	EMI	3	1

6.09.14: 43-30-84

Australia
20.11.05: **25**-37-46

Austria
20.11.05: **23**-29-38-51-63-64-64-53-71-72

Finland
12.11.05: 13-**2**-6-11-24-26-23-19-11-13-12-15-15-24

1.04.06: 40
20.01.07: 33-37

Germany
18.11.05: **3**-4-13-18-24-22-22-24-29-32-32-57-62-78-87-94

Italy
10.11.05: peaked at no.**9**, charted for 14 weeks

Japan
2.11.05: peaked at no.**53**, charted for 6 weeks

Netherlands

12.11.05: **7**-10-10-15-16-21-30-29-21-25-33-38-25-27-43-54-58-62-47-21-27-34-38-40-
  51-53-61-70-73-70-73-94-99-x-x-96

30.08.14: 100

New Zealand

14.11.05: **22**-31-40

Norway

12.11.05: **4**-9-14-20-22-25-21-12-13-21-30-x-39-x-24

Sweden

17.11.05: **7**-16-37-45-56-58-56-x-x-53

Switzerland

20.11.05: **12**-14-21-23-33-35-49-58-56-68-66

USA

26.11.05: **49**

AERIAL is Kate's eighth studio album ~ it was her first new album for 12 years, and her first double album.

Kate always intended to take a break, following *THE RED SHOES*, but for various reasons the gap grew and grew.

'Because they take such a long time,' said Kate, 'there's the impression that there are big gaps where I'm not doing anything, but with a lot of those records I was actually working on them for a long time ... I think I got to the point, at the end of the last one, where I just thought, "I don't want to go straight in and do another one. I want to take a break, and do some other stuff".'

Having ended her long-term relationship with Del Palmer, Kate married Dan McIntosh in 1992. Six years on, in July 1998, their son Albert ~ known as Bertie ~ was born. It wasn't until Bertie started school that Kate started thinking about and working on a new album.

'I think I live an extremely normal life,' said Kate, 'and it's something I've fought very hard to do. I don't choose to live my life in the industry ... I think I'm very privileged to be able to have my work as something that I love doing so much.'

The songs Kate composed for *AERIAL* were written between 1996 and 2005, and were recorded at London's Abbey Road Studios.

'I'm horrible to work with,' admitted Kate. 'I'm so fussy and picky. I think what's good is that I know what I want.'

AERIAL, like *HOUNDS OF LOVE* had been, was an album of two parts, which on this occasion were spread over two discs.

The first disc, titled 'A Sea of Honey' featured seven unrelated songs, but the second disc ~ 'A Sky Of Honey' ~ consisted of s single piece of music which speaks of outdoor adventures over a single summer's day.

The first disc, as well as the album's only single, *King Of The Mountain*, featured *Bertie*, a Renaissance-esque ode to Kate's young son, while *A Coral Room* was a stunning piano/vocal tribute to Kate's late mother, Hannah. The song *Joanni* took its inspiration from the story of Joan of Arc, while on π (Pi = the circumference of a circle divided by its diameter = 3.14159 ...) Kate sings the number to its 78th decimal place, and later in the song sings it from its 101st to its 137th decimal place.

Two songs on the second disc, *An Architect's Dream* and *The Painter's Link*, featured didgeridoo and spoken vocals by the soon-to-be-disgraced artist/singer, Rolf Harris. When *AERIAL* was remastered in 2018, Kate took the opportunity to edit Rolf Harris's spoken contribution, and replace his vocals with vocals by her son, Bertie.

AERIAL made its chart debut in the UK at no.3, behind Westlife's *FACE TO FACE* and Il Divo's new album, *ACORA*, which took the top spot. In other countries, *AERIAL* achieved no.2 in Finland, no.3 in Germany, no.4 in Norway, no.7 in the Netherlands and Sweden, no.9 in Italy, no.12 in Switzerland, no.22 in New Zealand, no.23 in Austria, no.25 in Australia, no.49 in the United States and no.53 in Japan.

10 ~ DIRECTOR'S CUT

Flower Of The Mountain/Song Of Solomon/Lily/Deeper Understanding/The Red Shoes/
This Woman's Work/Moments Of Pleasure/Never Be Mine/Top Of The City/And So Is
Love/Rubberband Girl

Produced by Kate Bush.

UK: Fish People FPCD 001 (2011).

28.05.11: **2**-11-30-53-60-98

Pos	LW	Title, Artist		Peak Pos	WoC
1	1	**21** ADELE	XL RECORDINGS	1	17
2	New	**DIRECTOR'S CUT** KATE BUSH	FISH PEOPLE	2	1
3	3	**19** ADELE	XL RECORDINGS	1	97

6.09.14: 44-50

Australia
5.06.11: **41**

Austria
27.05.11: **35**

Finland
21.05.11: **8**-20-28-48

Germany
27.05.11: **11**-14-45-69-80

Italy
26.05.11: peaked at no.**32**, charted for 3 weeks

Netherlands
21.05.11: **6**-19-22-26-45-63-72-82

New Zealand
23.05.11: **38**-39

Norway
14.05.11: 17-**2**-4-14-23-36

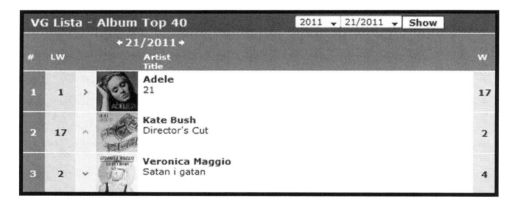

Spain
25.05.11: **71**

Sweden
27.05.11: **12**-44-50

Switzerland
29.05.11: **23**-48-92-81-96

Kate's first album for her own record label, which she called Fish People, was an album with a difference: it featured four tracks Kate had originally recorded for her 1989 album,

THE SENSUAL WORLD, together with seven tracks from 1993's *THE RED SHOES*. Kate completely re-recorded three songs ~ *Moments Of Pleasure*, *Rubberband Girl* and *This Woman's Work* ~ and re-worked the other tracks, with new vocals but largely maintaining the original instrumentation.

'For some time I have wanted to revisit tracks from these two albums,' she said, 'and that they could benefit from having new life breathed into them. Lots of work had gone into the original albums, and now these songs have another layer of work woven into them. I think of this as a new album.'

Back when she recorded *The Sensual World*, Kate had wanted to set the closing text from the James Joyce novel *Ulysses* to music, but was denied permission from Joyce's estate.

'When I came to work on this project,' said Kate, 'I thought I would ask permission again, and this time they said yes. It (*The Sensual World*) is now re-titled *Flower Of The Mountain*, and I am delighted that I have had the chance to fulfil the original concept.'

Kate worked on *DIRECTOR'S CUT* between 2009 and 2011, and the new version of *Deeper Understanding* was issued as a single, to help to promote the album. However, apart from spending a solitary week at no.87 in the UK and no.92 in France, the single wasn't a hit anywhere.

DIRECTOR'S CUT fared much better, entering the UK chart at no.2, behind Adele's mega-selling *21* album. The album also achieved no.2 in Norway, and charted at no.6 in the Netherlands, no.8 in Finland, no.11 in Germany, no.12 in Sweden, no.23 in Switzerland, no.32 in Italy, no.35 in Austria, no.38 in New Zealand and no.41 in Australia.

As well as digitally and as a standard CD in a case-bound book, *DIRECTOR'S CUT* was issued as a double vinyl album, and as a deluxe 'Collector's Edition', which included three CDs: *DIRECTOR'S CUT*, *THE SENSUAL WORLD* and *THE RED SHOES*.

11 ~ 50 WORDS FOR SNOW

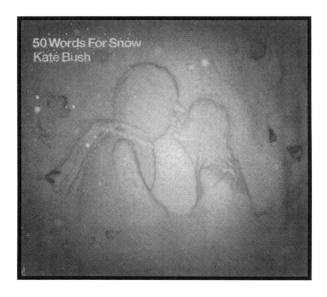

Snowflake/Lake Tahoe/Misty/Wild Man/Snowed In At Wheeler Street/50 Words For Snow/ Among Angels

Produced by Kate Bush.

UK: Fish People FPCD 007 (2011).

3.12.11: **5**-26-38-41-52-64-84-76-82
30.08.14: 83-20-31-76

Australia
4.12.11: **22**-42

Austria
2.12.11: **26**-56-70-73

Finland
19.11.11: 11-**8**-20-24-27-30-20-16-20-22-26-40

Germany
2.12.11: **7**-19-37-35-47-56-66-77-83

Italy
1.12.11: peaked at no.**38**, charted for 2 weeks

Netherlands
26.11.11: **10**-18-16-19-30-25-19-26-29-46-49-56-67-70

New Zealand
28.11.11: **39**

Norway
26.11.11: 18-**13**-26-38-38-36-31-29-22

Sweden
2.12.11: **13**-38-48-47-52-59-50-x-47

Switzerland
4.12.11: **12**-34-52-72-93

USA
10.12.11: **83**

After releasing just one new album between 1994 and 2010, Kate surprised and delighted her fans by releasing two albums in 2011.

Kate started working on the album that she titled *50 WORDS FOR SNOW* in 2010, and she recorded the album at London's Abbey Road Studios. Although it only featured seven songs, the album had a running time of 65 minutes. Every song on the album was well over six minutes, with *Lake Tahoe* topping 11 minutes and *Misty* clocking-in at 13:32 minutes. Kate was inspired to choose the album's title after thinking about the Eskimo people, who have fifty different words for snow.

On the opening track, *Snowflake*, Kate shared lead vocals with her son, Bertie. *Snowflake* leads into *Lake Tahoe*, where Kate is joined by choral singers Michael Wood and Stefan Roberts. Elton John trades vocals with Kate on *Snowed In At Wheeler Street*, and Stephen Fry ~ as Professor Joseph Yupik ~ joins Kate on the album's title track. The backing vocalist heard on *Wild Man* is Andy Fairweather-Low.

Wild Man, which was released as the lead and only single from *50 WORDS FOR SNOW* in most countries, tells the story of a group of explorers in the Himalayas who, having found evidence of the elusive Yeti, decide to cover up their find to protect the wild man. The single entered the UK chart at a lowly no.73, and slipped out of the Top 100 the following week. *Wild Man* wasn't a hit anywhere else.

In 2015, Kate remixed *Wild Man*, and contributed the resultant *Wild Man (Remastered Shimmer)* to the compilation album, *THE ART OF PEACE – SONGS FOR TIBET II*. The album marked the 80th birthday of the 14th Dalai Lama, and all proceeds from the album were donated to help to preserve the wisdom of the Dalai Lama and Tibetan culture in general.

In the UK, *Lake Tahoe* b/w *Among Angels* was exclusively issued as a limited edition 10" picture disc single in 2012, but it failed to chart.

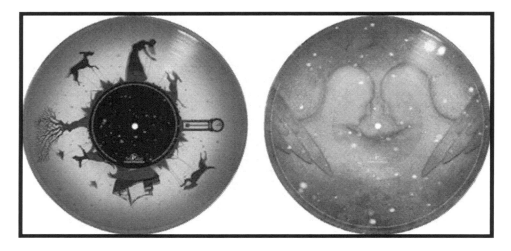

50 WORLDS FOR SNOW gave Kate her tenth Top 5 album in the UK, and achieved no.7 in Germany, no.8 in Finland, no.10 in the Netherlands, no.12 in Switzerland, no.13 in Norway and Sweden, no.22 in Australia, no.26 in Austria, no.38 in Italy and no.39 in New Zealand. The album also spent a week at no.83 on the Top 100 of the Billboard 200 in the United States.

12 ~ BEFORE THE DAWN

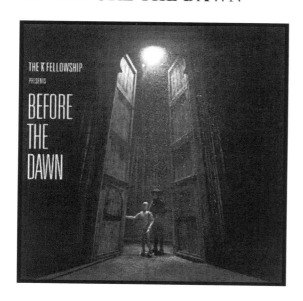

CD1 ~ Act I: *Lily/Hounds Of Love/Joanni/Top Of The City/Never Be Mine/Running Up That Hill (A Deal With God)/King Of The Mountain*

CD2 ~ Act II / The Ninth Wave: *Astronomer's Call (Spoken Monologue)/And Dream Of Sheep/Under Ice/Waking The Witch/Watching Them With Her (Dialogue)/Watching You Without Me/Little Light/Jig Of Life/Hello Earth/The Morning Fog*

CD3 ~ Act III: *Prelude/Prologue/The Architect's Dream/The Painter's Link/Sunset/Aerial Tal/Somewhere In Between/Tawny Moon/Nocturn/Aerial/Among Angels/Cloudbusting*

Produced by Kate Bush.

UK: Fish People 0190295920173 (2016).

8.12.16: **4**-23-28-28-55-81-78

Australia
11.12.16: **35**

Austria
9.12.16: **45**

Finland
3.12.16: **26**

Germany
2.12.16: **14**-56-68-x-x-x-x-81

Italy
1.12.16: **34**

Netherlands
3.12.16: **11**-39-50-61-80-90

Sweden
2.12.16: **45**

Switzerland
4.12.16: **37**-96

On 21st March 2014, via her website, Kate announced she was planning to perform live in concert for what would be the first time in 35 years. However, rather than embarking on a tour, Kate planned to play a 22 date residency at London's Hammersmith Apollo. The residency opened on 24th August 2014, with Kate's last show being staged on 1st October.

'It was an extraordinary experience putting the show together,' said Kate. 'It was a huge amount of work, a lot of fun and an enormous privilege to work with such an incredibly talented team.'

The team included Kate's son Bertie, who had just turned 16 years when the residency opened. As well as playing the part of the Painter and singing with the chorus, Bertie was credited as the show's creative advisor.

With one or two exceptions such as *Cloudbusting* apart, the Before The Dawn show focussed on Kate's more recent work, and didn't feature any of the songs she had recorded for her first four albums ~ so, to the disappointment of many fans, no *Wuthering Heights*. This didn't stop the residency from quickly selling out.

Kate's return to the stage generated enormous interest, and saw every one of her albums returning to the chart in the UK. On the chart dated 6th September 2014, Kate had an incredible 11 albums on the Top 50:

- no.6 ~ *THE WHOLE STORY*
- no.9 ~ *HOUNDS OF LOVE*
- no.20 ~ *50 WORDS FOR SNOW*
- no.24 ~ *THE KICK INSIDE*
- no.26 ~ *THE SENSUAL WORLD*
- no.37 ~ *THE DREAMING*
- no.38 ~ *NEVER FOR EVER*
- no.40 ~ *LIONHEART*
- no.43 ~ *AERIAL*
- no.44 ~ *DIRECTOR'S CUT*
- no.49 ~ *THE RED SHOES*

This was an unprecedented achievement for a female artist.

Two years after the residency ended, Kate released what was only her second live album, *BEFORE THE DAWN*. The first, *LIVE AT HAMMERSMITH ODEON*, was released as part of a box-set in 1994 ~ this comprised a home video of Kate's 1979 Tour of Life, which had originally been released in 1981, plus a CD version of the concert which hadn't been previously issued. *BEFORE THE DAWN* was credited to The KT Fellowship.

Like Kate's residency at the Hammersmith Apollo, *BEFORE THE DAWN* was split into three acts, which were each issued on a separate disc, making the release a triple CD album (the album was also released on four vinyl discs). One of the tracks from Act III, *Tawny Moon*, was performed by Kate's son, Bertie.

A promotional CD single, *And Dream Of Sheep*, was issued in Japan, the UK and the United States, but it wasn't a hit.

'This is the audio document,' said Kate, speaking prior to the release of *BEFORE THE DAWN*. 'I hope that this can stand alone as a piece of music in its own right, and that it can be enjoyed by people who knew nothing about the shows, as well as those who were there. I never expected the overwhelming response of the audiences, every night filling the show with life and excitement. They are there in every beat of the recorded music ~ even when you can't hear them, you can feel them.'

Given it was a relatively expensive triple live album, *BEFORE THE DAWN* did exceedingly well to enter the UK chart as high as no.4, thus giving Kate another Top 5 album. Kate, understandably, was thrilled by the album's success.

'A huge thank you to everyone who has supported the live album,' she said. 'It means so much to me, and for a triple live album to go into the charts at such a high position is just extraordinary.'

Outside the UK, although it couldn't match its UK success, *BEFORE THE DAWN* charted at no.11 in the Netherlands, no.14 in Germany, no.26 in Finland, no.34 in Italy, no.35 in Australia, no.37 in Switzerland, and no.45 in Austria and Sweden.

13 ~ REMASTERED PART I

Box-set of remastered editions of Kate's first seven studio albums:

- *THE KICK INSIDE*
- *LIONHEART*
- *NEVER FOR EVER*
- *THE DREAMING*
- *HOUNDS OF LOVE*
- *THE SENSUAL WORLD*
- *THE RED SHOES*

UK: Fish People 0190295569006 (2018).

29.11.18: **51**

Germany
23.11.18: **33**

Netherlands
24.11.18: **74**

Switzerland
25.11.18: **65**

As the title suggests, *REMASTERED PART I* was the first box-set to be released that featured remastered editions of Kate's back catalogue. The box-set comprised CD editions of Kate's first seven albums, from *THE KICK INSIDE* to *THE RED SHOES*, inclusive.

Box-sets, by their very nature, are far more expensive than standard albums, and they rarely chart. Kate's *REMASTERED PART I* did chart, although the only country where it achieved Top 40 status was Germany, where it spent one week at no.33. The box-set also charted for a solitary week in the UK, Switzerland and the Netherlands, at no.51, no.65 and no.74, respectively.

Two weeks after *REMASTERED PART I* appeared, Kate released *REMASTERED PART II*, a box-set of six CDs featuring remastered editions of Kate's more recent studio albums, *AERIAL, DIRECTOR'S CUT* and *50 WORDS FOR SNOW*, plus *BEFORE THE DAWN*, together with four CDs featuring 'The Other Sides', that is 12" Mixes, B-sides and Covers. This second box-set failed to achieve Top 40 status anywhere, but it did chart at no.64 in Germany and no.81 in the UK.

REMASTERED PART I & II were also issued on vinyl, but spread over four parts rather than two.

14 ~ THE OTHER SIDES

CD1 ~ 12" Mixes: *Running Up That Hill (A Deal With God)/The Big Sky (Meteorological Mix)/Cloudbusting (The Organon Mix)/Hounds Of Love (Alternative Mix)*

CD2 ~ The Other Side 1: *Walk Straight Down The Middle/You Want Alchemy/Be Kind To My Mistakes/Lyra/Under The Ivy/Experiment IV/Ne T'enfuis Pas/Un Baiser D'enfant/ Burning Bridge/Running Up That Hill (A Deal With God) (2012 Remix)*

CD3 ~ The Other Side 2: *Home For Christmas/One Last Look Around The House Before We Go/I'm Still Waiting/Warm And Soothing/Show A Little Devotion/Passing Through Air/Humming/Ran Tan Waltz/December Will Be Magic Again/Wuthering Heights (Remix/New Vocal From 'The Whole Story')*

CD4 ~ In Others' Words: *Rocket Man/Sexual Healing/Mna Ná Héireann/My Lagan Love/ The Man I Love/Brazil (Sam Lowry's First Dream)/The Handsome Cabin Boy/Lord Of The Reedy River/Candle In The Wind*

UK: Fish People 0190295568887 (2019).

21.03.19: **18**

Germany
15.03.19: **56**

The four CDs making up *THE OTHER SIDES* were originally released as part of Kate's 2018 box-set, *REMASTERED PART II*. The release featured one CD of 12" Mixes, two CDs of B-sides and one CD of Covers.

Released just a few months after *REMASTERED PART II*, *THE OTHER SIDES* sold well enough to enter the UK album chart at no.18, although it dropped off the Top 100 after just one week. *THE OTHER SIDES* also achieved no.56 in Germany, but it failed to chart in most countries.

KATE'S TOP 10 ALBUMS

This Top 10 has been compiled using the same points system as for the Top 20 Singles listing.

Rank/Album/Points

1   *HOUNDS OF LOVE* ~ 1545 points

2   *AERIAL* ~ 1221 points

3   *THE KICK INSIDE* ~ 1091 points

4   *THE SENSUAL WORLD* ~ 1084 points

5   *THE WHOLE STORY* ~ 1049 points

6. *50 WORDS FOR SNOW* ~ 960 points
7. *THE RED SHOES* ~ 956 points
8. *DIRECTOR'S CUT* ~ 889 points
9. *NEVER FOR EVER* ~ 784 points
10. *LIONHEART* ~ 757 points

Kate's 1985 album *HOUNDS OF LOVE* is her most successful release, followed by *AERIAL* and her debut, *THE KICK INSIDE. THE SENSUAL WORLD* and the 1986 compilation, *THE WHOLE STORY*, complete the Top 5.

    Kate's most recent album to make the Top 10 is *50 WORDS FOR SNOW*, which is at no.6.

ALBUMS TRIVIA

To date, Kate has achieved 14 Top 40 albums in one or more of the countries featured in this book.

There follows a country-by-country look at Kate's most successful albums, starting with her homeland.

KATE IN THE UK

Kate has achieved 15 hit albums in the UK, which spent 444 weeks on the Top 100.

No.1 Albums

1980	*NEVER FOR EVER*
1985	*HOUNDS OF LOVE*
1986	*THE WHOLE STORY*

Most weeks at No.1

3 weeks	*HOUNDS OF LOVE*
2 weeks	*THE WHOLE STORY*

Albums with the most weeks

145 weeks	*THE WHOLE STORY*
72 weeks	*THE KICK INSIDE*
67 weeks	*HOUNDS OF LOVE*
38 weeks	*LIONHEART*
25 weeks	*NEVER FOR EVER*
24 weeks	*THE SENSUAL WORLD*
24 weeks	*THE RED SHOES*
19 weeks	*AERIAL*
13 weeks	*50 WORDS FOR SNOW*
12 weeks	*THE DREAMING*

The Brit Certified/BPI (British Phonographic Industry) Awards

The BPI began certifying albums in 1973, and between April 1973 and December 1978, awards related to a monetary value and not a unit value. Thanks to inflation, this changed several times over the years:

- April 1973 – August 1974: Silver = £75,000, Gold = £150,000, Platinum = £1 million.
- September 1974 – December 1975: Gold raised to £250,000, others unchanged.
- January 1976 – December 1976: Silver raised to £100,000, others unchanged.
- January 1977 – December 1978: Silver raised to £150,000, Gold raised to £300,000, Platinum unchanged.

When this system was abolished, the awards that were set remain in place today: Silver = 60,000, Gold = 100,000, Platinum = 300,000. Multi-Platinum awards were introduced in February 1987.

In July 2013 the BPI automated awards, and awards from this date are based on actual sales since February 1994, not shipments.

4 x Platinum	*THE WHOLE STORY* (September 1994) = 1.2 million
2 x Platinum	*HOUNDS OF LOVE* (December 1986) = 600,000
Platinum	*THE KICK INSIDE* (May 1979) = 300,000
Platinum	*LIONHEART* (August 1980) = 300,000
Platinum	*THE SENSUAL WORLD* (October 1989) = 300,000
Platinum	*THE RED SHOES* (December 1993) = 300,000
Platinum	*AERIAL* (December 2005) = 300,000
Gold	*NEVER FOR EVER* (September 1980) = 100,000
Gold	*50 WORDS FOR SNOW* (December 2011) = 100,000
Gold	*DIRECTOR'S CUT* (December 2016) = 100,000
Gold	*BEFORE THE DAWN* (January 2017) = 100,000
Silver	*THE DREAMING* (December 1982) = 60,000

KATE IN AUSTRALIA

Kate has achieved 12 hit albums in Australia, which spent 162 weeks on the chart.

Her most successful album is *THE KICK INSIDE*, which peaked at no.3 in 1978.

Albums with the most weeks

41 weeks	*THE KICK INSIDE*
28 weeks	*THE WHOLE STORY*
20 weeks	*NEVER FOR EVER*
19 weeks	*HOUNDS OF LOVE*
18 weeks	*LIONHEART*
10 weeks	*THE DREAMING*

KATE IN AUSTRIA

Kate has achieved six hit albums in Austria, which spent 34 weeks on the chart.

Her most successful album is *HOUNDS OF LOVE*, which peaked at no.14 in 1985.

Albums with the most weeks

14 weeks	*HOUNDS OF LOVE*
10 weeks	*AERIAL*
4 weeks	*THE RED SHOES*
4 weeks	*50 WORDS FOR SNOW*

KATE IN BELGIUM (Flanders)

Since 1995, when the album chart was launched, Kate has achieved six hit albums in Belgium (Flanders), which spent 39 weeks on the chart.

Her most successful album is *AERIAL*, which peaked at no.11.

Albums with the most weeks

20 weeks	*AERIAL*
11 weeks	*50 WORDS FOR SNOW*
5 weeks	*DIRECTOR'S CUT*

KATE IN CANADA

Kate has achieved nine hit albums in Canada, which spent 152 weeks on the chart.

Her most successful album is *HOUNDS OF LOVE*, which peaked at no.7 in 1985.

Albums with the most weeks

45 weeks	*HOUNDS OF LOVE*
23 weeks	*THE WHOLE STORY*
22 weeks	*THE SENSUAL WORLD*
17 weeks	*THE DREAMING*
17 weeks	*THE RED SHOES*
9 weeks	*KATE BUSH*
8 weeks	*ON STAGE* EP

FREE 11-TRACK **CD** NEW PROG MUSIC

KATE BUSH's NEVER FOR EVER

PROG

ASTOUNDING SOUNDS AMAZING

In the charts and in control: the album that changed everything

+

TEARS FOR FEARS
KEVIN GODLEY
DYBLE LONGDON
JAKKO JAKSZYK
GAZPACHO
MOTORPSYCHO

JOHN PETRUCCI
Reunites with Mike Portnoy on new solo album

AYREON
Dutch proggers release their craziest concept album ever

EDDIE JOBSON
Tales of Tull, Zappa, Curved Air, Roxy, UK and more…

FUTURE

KATE BUSH is a 5- or 6- track mini-album released exclusively in North America:

Sat In Your Lap/James And The Cold Gun (Live Version)/Ne T'Enfuis Pas/ Babooshka/Suspended In Gaffa/Un Baiser D'Enfant (The Infant Kiss

Ne T'Enfuis Pas Was omitted from the American edition of the mini-album. In Canada, as well as the standard black vinyl edition, the mini-album was issued on blue, brown, clear, green, orange (gold) and white vinyl.

Note: Kate's *On Stage* EP was classed as an album in Canada.

KATE IN FINLAND

Kate has achieved ten hit albums in Finland, which spent 111 weeks on the chart.

Her most successful album is *THE KICK INSIDE*, which peaked at no.2.

Albums with the most weeks

27 weeks	*THE KICK INSIDE*
17 weeks	*AERIAL*
14 weeks	*HOUNDS OF LOVE*
13 weeks	*THE RED SHOES*
12 weeks	*50 WORDS FOR SNOW*
12 weeks	*THE SENSUAL WORLD*

KATE IN FRANCE

Kate has achieved eight hit albums in France, which spent 46 weeks on the chart.

Her highest charting album is *THE WHOLE STORY*, which peaked at no.9 on the Compilations chart.

Albums with the most weeks

21 weeks	*AERIAL*
8 weeks	*HOUNDS OF LOVE*
4 weeks	*THE SENSUAL WORLD*
4 weeks	*THE WHOLE STORY*
4 weeks	*50 WORDS FOR SNOW*

KATE IN GERMANY

Kate has achieved 15 hit albums in Germany, which spent 184 weeks on the chart.

Her most successful album is *HOUNDS OF LOVE*, which peaked at no.2.

Albums with the most weeks

32 weeks	*HOUNDS OF LOVE*
31 weeks	*NEVER FOR EVER*
21 weeks	*THE SENSUAL WORLD*
19 weeks	*THE DREAMING*
19 weeks	*THE WHOLE STORY*
16 weeks	*AERIAL*
10 weeks	*THE KICK INSIDE*
10 weeks	*THE RED SHOES*

KATE IN ITALY

Kate has achieved six hit albums in Italy, which spent 39 weeks on the chart.

Her most successful album is *AERIAL*, which peaked at no.9 in 2005.

Albums with the most weeks

14 weeks	*THE SENSUAL WORLD*

14 weeks	*AERIAL*
13 weeks	*THE KICK INSIDE*

KATE IN JAPAN

Kate has achieved 10 hit albums in Japan, which spent 80 weeks on the chart.

Her highest charting album is *THE SENSUAL WORLD*, which peaked at no.18 in 1989.

Albums with the most weeks

14 weeks	*THE KICK INSIDE*
13 weeks	*LIONHEART*
11 weeks	*HOUNDS OF LOVE*
10 weeks	*THE WHOLE STORY*
8 weeks	*NEVER FOR EVER*

Note: Kate's *On Stage* EP was classed as an album in Japan.

KATE IN THE NETHERLANDS

Kate has achieved 13 hit albums in the Netherlands, which spent 243 weeks on the chart.

No.1 Albums

1878	*THE KICK INSIDE*
1985	*HOUNDS OF LOVE*

Both albums topped the chart for two weeks.

Albums with the most weeks

46 weeks	*HOUNDS OF LOVE*
37 weeks	*THE WHOLE STORY*
34 weeks	*AERIAL*
30 weeks	*THE KICK INSIDE*
18 weeks	*NEVER FOR EVER*
14 weeks	*THE SENSUAL WORLD*
14 weeks	*50 WORDS FOR SNOW*
13 weeks	*THE RED SHOES*
12 weeks	*LIONHEART*
10 weeks	*THE DREAMING*

KATE IN NEW ZEALAND

Kate has achieved 10 hit albums in New Zealand, which spent 103 weeks on the chart.

Her most successful album is *THE KICK INSIDE*, which peaked at no.2 in 1978.

Albums with the most weeks

30 weeks	*THE KICK INSIDE*
22 weeks	*THE WHOLE STORY*
20 weeks	*HOUNDS OF LOVE*
12 weeks	*NEVER FOR EVER*
10 weeks	*LIONHEART*

KATE IN NORWAY

Kate has achieved 10 hit albums in Norway, which spent 111 weeks on the chart.

Her highest charting albums are *NEVER FOR EVER* and *DIRECTOR'S CUT*, which both peaked at no.2.

Albums with the most weeks

25 weeks	*THE KICK INSIDE*
20 weeks	*NEVER FOR EVER*
15 weeks	*LIONHEART*
13 weeks	*AERIAL*
9 weeks	*50 WORDS FOR SNOW*

KATE IN SOUTH AFRICA

None of Kate's albums have charted in South Africa.

KATE IN SPAIN

Only one of Kate's albums, *DIRECTOR'S CUT*, has charted in Spain ~ it spent a solitary week at no.71 in 2011.

KATE IN SWEDEN

Kate has achieved 12 hit albums in Sweden, which spent 64 weeks on the chart.

Her highest charting album is *AERIAL*, which peaked at no.7 in 2005.

Albums with the most weeks

10 weeks	*THE KICK INSIDE*
8 weeks	*AERIAL*
8 weeks	*50 WORDS FOR SNOW*
5 weeks	*LIONHEART*
5 weeks	*HOUNDS OF LOVE*
5 weeks	*THE SENSUAL WORLD*

KATE IN SWITZERLAND

Kate has achieved eight hit albums in Switzerland, which spent 46 weeks on the chart.

Her most successful album is *HOUNDS OF LOVE*, which peaked at no.3 in 1985.

Albums with the most weeks

12 weeks	*HOUNDS OF LOVE*
11 weeks	*AERIAL*
5 weeks	*THE SENSUAL WORLD*
5 weeks	*THE RED SHOES*
5 weeks	*DIRECTOR'S CUT*
5 weeks	*50 WORDS FOR SNOW*

KATE IN THE USA

Kate has achieved six hit albums in the United States, which spent 66 weeks on the Top 100 of the Billboard 200.

Her highest charting album is *HOUNDS OF LOVE*, which peaked at no.12 in 2022.

Albums with the most weeks

31 weeks	*HOUNDS OF LOVE*
20 weeks	*THE SENSUAL WORLD*
10 weeks	*THE WHOLE STORY*

RIAA (Recording Industry Association of America) Awards

The RIAA began certifying Gold albums in 1958, Platinum albums in 1976, and multi-Platinum albums in 1984. Gold = 500,000, Platinum = 1 million. Awards are based on shipments, not sales, and each disc is counted individually (so, for example, a double album has to ship 500,000 to be eligible for Platinum).

Gold   *THE SENSUAL WORLD* (October 1993) = 500,000